Woman Who Has Sprouted Wings: Poems By Contemporary Latin American Women Poets

Edited by
Mary Crow

LATIN AMERICAN LITERARY REVIEW PRESS
SERIES: DISCOVERIES
PITTSBURGH, PENNSYLVANIA 1984

The Latin American Literary Review Press publishes Latin American creative writing under the series title Discoveries and critical works under the series title Explorations.

This project is partially supported by a grant from the National Endowment for the Arts in Washington, D.C., a Federal agency.

While still in manuscript, this anthology won a Translation Award from the Translation Center of Columbia University.

Library of Congress Cataloging in Publication Data.

Main entry under title:

Woman who has sprouted wings.

Chiefly English and Spanish with some Portuguese.
1. Latin American poetry—Women authors—Translations into English. 2. Latin American poetry—20th century— Translations into English. 3. English poetry—Translations from Spanish. 4. English poetry—Translations from Portuguese. 5. Latin American poetry. I. Crow, Mary.
PQ7087.E5W65 1983   861'.009'9287   84-5672
ISBN 0-935480-14-5

Woman Who Has Sprouted Wings: Poems By Contemporary Latin American Women Poets can be ordered directly from the publisher, Latin American Literary Review Press, P.O. Box 8385, Pittsburgh, Pennsylvania 15218.

Cover design by Phil Risbeck.

ACKNOWLEDGMENTS

Marjorie Agosin. DELIA DOMINGUEZ, "The Blue Bottles", "I Read Fortunes in Dreams," and "The Sun Looks Back," used by permission of the translator. "The Blue Bottles" and "The Sun Looks Back" originally appeared in *Colorado State Review* (Spring 1982).

Maureen Ahern. ROSARIO CASTELLANOS, "Empty House," "Silence Near a Stone," "Malinche," and "Home Economics," used by permission of the translator. "Malinche" first appeared in *Colorado State Review* (Fall 1979). The other three translations first appeared in a chapbook, *Looking at the Mona Lisa* (© Revelin / Ecuatorial, London, 1981).

Claribel Alegría, "Flores del Volcán," "Tamalitos de Cambray," and "Soy espejo," used by permission of the poet.

Lynne Alvarez. ALEJANDRA PIZARNIK, "From the Other Side," "From a Copy of 'Les Chants de Maldoror'," and "Exile" used by permission of the translator. "Exile" is reprinted from Octavio Armand, *Toward an Image of Latin American Poetry* (© Logbridge-Rhodes, Durango, Co., 1982).

Carlos and Monique Altschul. RENATA PALLOTTINI, "That Night, "Message," "The Shriek," and "To Write," permission of translators. "The Shriek" first appeared in *Colorado State Review* (Fall/Winter 1980). "Message" is reprinted from *Women Poets of the World* (© Macmillan, New York, 1983).

Patsy Boyer. CIRCE MAIA, "Where There Used to be Badlands," "Possibilities," "Wet Grapes . . . ," "Let's Go Again," "Going Out," and "A Wind Will Come from the South." Translated with Mary Crow and used by permission of the author. "Wet Grapes" previously appeared in *Colorado State Review* (Fall 1979) and was reprinted in *Cut-*

bank (Spring/Summer 1980) which also published "A Wind Will Come from the South." "Possibilities" first appeared in *Grove* (Spring 1982).

Cecilia Bustamante, "Bajo el sol," "Resonancias," "Despierta," and "El astronauta," are used by permission of the poet.

Pamela Carmell. RAQUEL JODOROWSKY, "Poem in Every Language," "Jellyfish," The Power of Mankind," "Song for Vocal Chords and Instruments of Electronic Crying," permission to publish granted by the translator. "Poem in Every Language" first appeared in *Chouteau Review* (Fall 1983); "Jellyfish" in *International Poetry Review* (Spring 1983); "Song . . ." in *Colorado State Review* (Spring 1980).

María Mercedes Carranza, "De Boyaca en los campos," "Erase una mujer a una virtud pegada," "Patas arriba con la vida," used by permission of poet.

Mary Crow. MARIA MERCEDES CARRANZA, "Once Upon a Time a Woman Tied to a Virtue" and "Heels over Head with Life" re-printed by permission of *Grove* (Spring 1982), where they were first published, and the translator. CECILIA BUSTAMANTE, "Under the Sun," "Awake," and "The Astronaut." "Under the Sun" and "The Astronaut" first appeared in *Grove* (Spring 1982). CIRCE MAIA, "Where There Used to be Badlands," "Possibilities," Wet Grapes . . . ," "Let's Go Again," and "A Wind Will Come from the South," translated with Patsy Boyer and used by permission of the author. "Possibilities" first appeared in *Grove* (Spring 1982); "Wet Grapes," *Colorado State Review* (Fall 1979); "A Wind Will Come from the South" and "Wet Grapes" (re-printed) in *Cutbank* (Spring/Summer 1980).

Delia Domínguez, "Los Frascos Azules," "El Sol mira para atrás," and "Adivino los sueños," re-printed by permission of the poet.

John Felstiner. VIOLETA PARRA, "Goddamn the Empty Sky," re-printed from *Colorado State Review* (Fall/Winter 1980), and used by permission of the translator.

Darvin J. Flakoll. CLARIBEL ALEGRÍA, "Flowers from the Volcano," "Little Cambric Tamales," "I'm a Mirror," used by permission of the translator. *Colorado State Review* (Fall 1979) first printed the translation of "Flowers from the Volcano."

Fondo de Cultura Economica. ROSARIO CASTELLANOS, "Silencio cerca de una piedra antigua" "La casa vacía," "Malinche," and "Economía domestica," all re-printed by permission of Fondo de cultura económica, México City.

Rita Geada, "Para que ardar," "Devolvedme mi mundo," "En el aquelarre," used by permission of the poet.

Ulalume González de Leon, "Las sabanas familiares," ")Parentesis(," "Mariposa Amarilla," "Discontinuidad," and "Jardin Escrito," used by permission of poet.

Raquel Jodorowsky, "El poder del hombre," "Las Malaquas," "Canción para cuerdas de garganta e instrumentos de llanto electronico," "Poema en todos los idiomas," used by permission of poet.

Macmillan Publishing Co., Inc., permission granted for re-publication of paragraphs by Mary Crow from Introduction to section on "Latin America," © Women Poets of the World (Macmillan, New York, 1983), and the translations of four poems quoted in the text of that introduction.

Circe Maia, "Donde había barrancas," "Posibilidades," "Mojadas uvas . . .," "Vamonos de nuevo," "Vendrá un viento del sur," used by permission of poet.

Nancy Morejón, "A un muchacho," "hay el calor," and "Masacre," used by permission of poet.

Sara Nelson. ULALUME GONZALEZ DE LEON, "Familiar Sheets," "Yellow Butterfly," "Discontinuity," used by permission of the translator. "Yellow Butterfly" and "Discontinuity" originally appeared in Colorado State Review (Spring 1980).

Renata Pallotini, "Naguela Noite," "O Grito," "Mensagem," and "Escrever," used by permission of the poet.

Violeta Parra, "Run-Run se fue pa'l norte," "Según el favor del viento," and "Maldigo del alto cielo," used by permission of the poet's heirs.

Susan Pensak. ALEJANDRA PIZARNIK "Childhood," "Primitive Eyes," and "The Understanding," used by permission of the translator.

5

TABLE OF CONTENTS

Preface 9
General Introduction 15
Alejandra Pizarnik (translated by Lynne Alvarez; Susan Pensak) —
Argentina 29
Renata Pallottini (translated by Monique and
Carlos Altschl) — Brazil 39
Delia Domínguez (translated by Marjorie Agosín) — Chile 49
Violeta Parra (tanslated by Bonnie Shepard; John
Felstiner) — Chile 57
María Mercedes Carranza (translated by
Mary Crow; Ellen Watson) — Colombia 71
Rita Geada (translated by Donald Walsh) — Cuba 79
Nancy Morejón (translated by Heather Sievert) — Cuba 85
Rosario Castellanos (translated by Maureen Ahern) — Mexico 93
Ulalume González de León (translated by Sara
Nelson; Eliot Weinberger) — Mexico 107
Cecilia Bustamante (translated by Mary Crow;
David Tipton) — Peru 121
Raquel Jodorowsky (translated by Pamela Carmell) — Peru 131
Claribel Alegría (translated by Darwin J. Flakoll) —
El Salvador 141
Circe Maia (translated by Patsy Boyer and Mary Crow) —
Uruguay 155
María Sabina (translated by Henry Munn) — Mexico 167

PREFACE

A woman poet is seen as an anomaly. It has been said many times in the last decade but it has to be said again, because, today as yesterday, female creativity is still perceived as aggression, rivalry, or thwarted sexuality. Still one hears people say that Emily Dickinson found an ersatz satisfaction in her poetry because, poor thing, she was unable to find a man and that Alfonsina Storni, the Argentinian poet, was too ugly to be loved and so, killed herself. This trivialization of female experience, of the life and work of women poets, so permeates the culture that, even today, women poets remain invisible. Well intended, and not so well intended, compilers of anthologies of poetry, especially of poetry in translation, overlook the women again and again. To be sure, the habit of reading foreign poetry is a fairly recent phenomenon, but it arose side by side with feminism in the late 60's and 70's and should have been affected by it. Yet important anthologies are being published this very day with, at best, a single woman poet.

As a result of this peculiar blindness we now have a situation where many foreign male poets, especially Latin American, are known and appreciated in this country, while women poets remain virtually unknown. Most poetry readers are familiar with Neruda, Vallejo, or Carlos Drummond de Andrade but have never read a line of poetry by a Latin American woman poet, with the exception maybe of Gabriela Mistral. A prolonged and intense effort will be necessary in order to redress this imbalance and bring the work of women poets to the attention of readers of poetry.

Two international anthologies which I was involved in editing myself, THE OTHER VOICE and WOMEN POETS OF THE WORLD, were efforts of this kind. So is this fine collection of Latin American women poets. The editor, Mary Crow, has introduced us to a group of outstanding contemporary poets, many of whom have never before appeared in English translation. Presented this way, within the framework of a single volume, the seriousness, the weight of the poetry, is immediately apparent, even to a casual reader. These poets will have to be reckoned with by those dealing with Latin American poetry in the future.

But an anthology like this one does more than simply create a platform for women poets. Each process of selecting and grouping brings out different

9

aspects in the poetry. The poets in this book are female. They have female bodies and female sensibilities. They were raised as girls and had female role models and expectations impressed on them. Their experience of the world—in work, love, friendship—was colored by the fact that they were women. When they sat down to write poetry they did not forget that they were women, they did not move out of their bodies nor divest themselves of their female experiences.

It is hard to imagine what it is like to be a woman and a poet in Latin America. Life must be governed by innumerable rules and taboos. If the women are protected they are at the same time excluded from most areas of active life. Outside, in the full heat of the sun, there must be the life of "telegrams and anger" in which men move freely, while indoors, behind thick white-washed walls and closed shutters, the women glide past like shadows. The imagination strains, grasps at clichés and tries to put together a picture out of fragments of movies, novels, scenes glimpsed during travels. But the wonderful thing about poetry, about the voice of the individual poet, is that it is capable of reaching beyond the cliches and bringing that alien reality close to us. In reading the poems we become able to imagine that distant reality in all its specificity.

At times the poet's voice speaks to us intimately of that very peculiar feminine experience of being reduced to silence.

> We have resolved not to exist. Or rather
> it has been resolved that we do not exist.
> So we stay quiet, deep down,
> doing nothing.
>
> Like children too good
> who have quit playing in order not to make noise
> and neither talk nor read because there are rustlings
> when the pages turn.
>   Circe Maia (Uruguay)

The feeling is conveyed as experienced from within, in the form of interiorized repression eating away at the sense of self and reducing it to nothing, the inner voice muffled, existence snuffed out for lack of air. This must be what Thoreau was thinking of when he said about the Concord peasant that he was leading a life of quiet desperation; rage and frustration seething under the placid surface. But Thoreau's peasant would at times give vent to his rage by striking his mare, his children, or his wife. The women in Circe Maia's poem have no such outlet for the overflow of feelings. Anger and desperation erupt in unexpected and mute ways,

in the form of silent stabs.
A thought-needle, voice-splinter
utters the inaudible scream: "Still!"

In another poem the anger bursts forth disguised as self-denigration. We recognize the tone, the familiar tone of self-hatred that comes from knowing that one's life, the only one there is, has been reduced to this or that role, a stereotype, fit for cheap melodrama.

Now I am a woman
of easy virtue,
a woman lost: I perform
all my duties
I am a well
of kindness, I breathe
holiness
from every pore.

María Mercedes Carranza (Colombia)

Violeta Parra brings a different voice into the book. Maybe because she was poor and had to make a living singing in bars and other public places, because she was not shut up in middle-class conventions and proprieties, there is none of that airless, claustral atmosphere of stunted selves and mute rage in her poems. That doesn't mean the poems are happy; that she is free to move in the world outside does not mean that she automatically had access to the intoxicating air of a life of action and power. The outside world she saw and wrote poems about was wrought with hopeless poverty and misery, day after day, generation after generation.

This is no life—the Chilote's—
no schooling, no courts,
ragged shoes for their feet
potatoes and garlic to eat
hard wood to keep warm
from the government's cold, I cry,
their bones are breaking,
I'm going, I'm going.
. . .
The Chilotes all in black
inside more than out
with their plate of hope
and their blanket of sky

begging the mountain
for their bitter bread, I cry
at the mercy of the wind,
I'm going. I'm going.

Her compassion can do so little. She stands so utterly helpless in front of all this misery. What does the cry signify? Despair or defiance? Or both? It is truly a miracle, though, the way the voice of the poet brings that distant world within the range of our understanding and our emotions, how it stirs in us the same helpless anger, the same compassion.

Violeta Parra died by suicide in 1967. It makes one wonder how other poets manage to live from day to day in Chile, in Argentina, in El Salvador. How do they manage to live in the midst of the razzias, the round ups, the sudden disappearances of husbands, friends, sons, brothers? How does one go on laughing and living, planting a garden or buying new shoes while there are rumors of distant killings and, on certain mornings, the sudden appearance of a corpse in the ditch that no one dares to claim? How does one manage to write poetry under such conditions?

For some, it seems, poetry becomes a necessity, a way of carrying on and keeping going and something of a sacred mission. Poetry becomes

signs on tree bark
letters on elusive paper,
so this puny flame,
lightning, will o' the wisp,
will not go dark
                    Renata Pallottini (Brazil)

It is vital that someone remember and record what is happening and pass the knowledge on to future generations.

Tell your son, my son,
that we endured:
there were taped confessions
and pictures full face.
Tell how we shrunk
like beaten beasts;
that nobody had the courage,
that we breathed in shame,
eyes fleeing other eyes,
hands cold and sweating.
                    R.P.

Typically, what is passed on here is not the heroic deed, the grand gesture of romantic bravura. The poet is a woman and she knows that a decent life, a life worth living, is impossible without peace and order and stability. Civil war brings out the worst in us: fear, cunning, and brutality. Tender human feelings evaporate, the most thick-skinned survive. The effect of torture is always degrading, on the victim as well as on the executioner.

When the women poets in these pages turn to contemporary history, to what is happening in Latin America now, they often side, not with the revolutionaries or preservers of status quo, not with this or that ideology, but with those who survived and endured. They side with the ones they love and who are now dead,

> No one can say
> how they died.
> Their silenced voices are one silence.
> My dead arise, they rage.
> The streets are empty but my dead
> wink at me.
> I am a cemetery.
> I have no country.
> They are too many to bury.
>
> Claribel Alegría (El Salvador)

Sometimes they side with those who managed to carry with them the last spark of hope, however futile and naive it might appear under the circumstances. Their poetry is a little like the blue bottles in a poem by Delia Domínguez. Nobody knows what the blue bottles were supposed to be used for. They were passed on from hand to hand. One legend has it that they were brought to the new world by a colonist who set sail from Hamburg one hundred fifty years ago. There are other legends as well, but no one knows for sure that the bottles are ever going to be of any use. Yet the poet has taken special care in preserving these fragile and useless blue bottles, for, as she says

> In the blue bottles I keep the air
> that I'll give to you someday
> when everything comes true.

JOANNA BANKIER

INTRODUCTION

This collection of poems by Latin American women poets has been a long time in the making, for my first attempts to locate poets and to gather poems were tentative and groping. Indeed, when I first began in 1976 to look for the work of Latin American women poets, I could find only a few names, a few poems. Like many other poets writing in the U.S., I had long been impressed by the energy and power of the poems of male Latin American poets available here through translations. The poems of César Vallejo, Pablo Neruda, Octavio Paz, Nicanor Parra, and Nicolás Guillén were frequently discussed over coffee or wine as well as in classrooms and workshops, and their work served as model and inspiration. And the Latin American fiction writers also had their impact on poetry—especially Gabriel García Márquez, Julio Cortázar, Jorge Luis Borges, Carlos Fuentes, José Donoso. All of these authors were part of the widespread literary renaissance that has developed in Latin America in the twentieth century and influenced U.S. poetry. What concerned me was that Latin American women's voices weren't being heard, with the possible exception of Gabriela Mistral who had won the Nobel Prize for Literature in 1945. I wondered about a twentieth century literary renaissance in which women seemed to have little or no part, especially since in the past decade in the U.S. so many North American women poets had really begun to be heard. When I had the chance for a sabbatical leave from Colorado State University in 1976-77, I decided to set out to see if I could discover what role women poets had actually had, and were having, in the Latin American boom.

In the U.S., the new tradition of women poets culminated in the 70's with such an explosion of women writers that their work, or articles about it, fills entire magazines (such as *The Second Wave, Best Friends, Woman Poet, Calyx, The 13th Moon, Aphra, Helicon Nine, Sing Heavenly Muse*), magazines which span a considerable range of editorial philosophy from the requirement that material be radical feminist or radical lesbian to no requirement except that the author be a woman. Moreover, anthologies comprised entirely of women poets are common, and even general anthologies usually present the reader with a selection of women poets. Feminist presses publish books of individual women's poetry, and both the small presses and the commercial presses are more open to the publication of women writers. In every part of the country, women read their poems to receptive audiences.

This increased number of outlets, combined with women's poetry workshops, courses on women writers, and informal support groups, has fostered women writers' efforts and encouraged the confidence, discipline, experimentation, and revision necessary to creative growth. Discussion of the feminine voice and principles of a feminist criticism have freed women from various traditions and given them the hope of their own originality and their own language. The result, of course, is that in this country there are more and more fine women poets, no matter what standard of judgment is used. Women have gained confidence, and confidence has helped them to write and to make public their writings.

Unfortunately, these processes have not yet taken hold in Latin America. Women poets there can point to the great women poets of earlier generations and know that some women have succeeded—against great odds. Against these odds, exceptional women have succeeded as poets from at least as early as the 17th century, when the mysterious "Amarilis" was writing epistolary verse in Peru and Sor Juana Inés de la Cruz was writing in dozens of verse forms in Mexico (to the displeasure of the Church which finally silenced her). Much, much earlier, there undoubtedly were women poets among the indigenous Indians. How many we will never know.

Clearly, in the early Indian cultures with their tight class structures and dependence on physical labor, the women who could have access to the education and leisure necessary for the composition of poetry would tend to be women of the upper classes or concubines of men in the upper classes, on the one hand, and shamanesses or priestesses, on the other. An example of a woman poet from among the Aztecs of the Middle Ages about whom some records exist is Macuilxochitl, a princess born in about 1435 at Tenochtitlan. Rich, well educated, trained in the crafts, she was the daughter of Tlacaelel, called by the Aztec historian, "conqueror of the world." She lived in a period of warfare and sang the praises of Aztec warriors:

> Slowly he presents offering
> of flowers and feathers
> to the Giver of Life.
> He puts eagle crests
> on the arms of men,
> there where war burns
> in the interior of the plains.
> Like our songs,
> like our flowers,
> so, you, warrior with cropped head,
> you give happiness to the Giver of Life.

Her song is a celebration: "I raise up my songs, / I, Macuilxochitl, / with them I make the Giver of Life happy, / May the dance begin!"

That shamanesses existed not only in pre-Colombian times but through history and that they composed oral poetry seems likely—if only on the evidence of their existence today and the persistence of Indian social structures down the centuries. In a chapter about women's roles in "Earliest Civilizations," Ferdinand Anton, in his study, *Women in Pre-Colombian America,* says, "There was not yet any organized caste of priests, but the small figures and masks give proof of the existence of shamans, probably some of them female."

A number of such female shamans have existed in modern times and a few have had their poems or chants recorded, most notably María Sabina, a Mazatec shaman of Mexico, who is the subject of several books. A study has been made of the Mapuche Indian *machi* (Shaman) women, but it has been recorded only on film and tape and is not available to the general reader. Among the Quechuas today, an oral tradition of courtship poems exists, and it is at least possible that some women have shown talent in composing such poems. Unfortunately, relatively few transcriptions of oral poems by native Latin American women exist, and it is impossible to judge how much has been lost. Thus, it is difficult to judge how typical María Sabina's endless chant is. Its tremendous energy and assertive spirit led me to choose it as epigraph and ending for this book.

Just as we know practically nothing of the Latin American native women poets of today, we will almost certainly never learn anything about the native women poets of the past. Their work, if it existed, is lost, and the work of contemporaries remains undiscovered. We are not yet sufficiently geared to the translation of the oral literatures of indigenous languages to recover whatever there is.

Until we know more about the lives of Latin American women in all walks and times, we can only begin to address the problems and successes of women who wanted to create poetry. However, the gaining of such knowledge is complicated because so many different countries are involved and few scholars or critics can hope to speak with equal authority of all—countries as diverse as the heavily Indian Andean nations of Bolivia and Peru, and the Europeanized southern nations of Uruguay and Argentina, and, within those countries, Indian groups as diverse as the Yucatan Mayans of Mexico and the Guaranis of Paraguay.

For these reasons, the task of knowing Latin American women's poetry must, for the moment, focus on the poetry written in Spanish from the conquest to the present. The earliest great woman poet of Latin America, Sor Juana Inés de la Cruz (1651-1695), is much written about today because her life demonstrates both how exceptional and difficult it was for a Latin

American woman of literary talent to emerge in past centuries and how genius may blossom even under adverse circumstances. Sor Juana was precocious enough to read at three, a woman of renaissance accomplishments: learned in languages, sciences, and the arts; a skilled speaker and writer; trained in philosophy and religion. Her poetry demonstrates virtually every form common in her time, most of the techniques and ornaments. Most frequently her poems deal with religious themes, but in one famous poem, she attacks men for blaming women for female weakness which she says is the fault of men themselves who control women. Her absorption in books and poetry was increasingly seen as dangerous by the church, and, after several warnings, she finally gave up reading and writing and devoted herself wholly to the self-denial and self-castigation of the religious life.

After Sor Juana, other women of the upper classes wrote occasional and spiritual verse, generally lacking in originality (but no worse than the work of most Latin American male poets of their time) for they lived during the long period of imitation of Spain. Typical and a little better than average was Sor Francisca del Castillo y Guevara (1671-1742) of Colombia, writer of mystical verse whose exactitude in doctrine was praised along with the tenderness, simplicity, and transparency of her style.

By the 19th century, a number of women were writing poetry. As early as 1875, an anthology presented 50 women poets writing on the conventional themes—children, parents, home, nature, and religion. However, out of all the women writing poetry in Latin America in the 19th century, only one has retained a place in literary history: Gertrudis Gómez de Avellaneda (1814-1873), considered one of the important figures of Spanish romanticism. When she was 22, her family moved from Cuba to Spain, and it was in Spain that she wrote her poems, novels, plays, and translations. Treating her life as a model for other women, she wrote autobiographical poems, plays, and novels. She wrote voluminously presenting women as both strong characters and as victims. She was interested in the work of other women writers, especially of Madame de Stael and George Sand, and in the unconventional lives they led. She criticized the sexist ideas and customs of her time. In her era, only Avellaneda among Latin American women writers was able to become a part of the masculine literary scene.

If Latin American literature finally cast free of Spain's dominance in 1888 with the publication of Rubén Darío's *Azul* and the introduction of *modernismo* to the new world, the work of women poets was not at first touched by this excitement and change. Women continued to write on the old themes in the old style for several decades. Nonetheless, a woman born near the end of the 19th century raised a voice early in the 20th century that is considered by many to be the voice of the first original Latin American woman poet. That poet was Delmira Augustini.

Delmira Augustini (1886-1914) combines the erotic and the intellectual in her work, the expression of her search for the ideal love.

> —I don't want more life than your life,
> there are in you the supreme elements.
> Leave me below the sky of your body!

In spite of the fact that her city, Montevideo, was a cosmopolitan city, her work barely reflects the exciting literary movements current in Europe and known in the new world via travellers. Only occasionally do her poems break free of their naive romanticism, and we have a subtle and symbolist poem like "The Swan":

> Blue pupil of my park
> is the sensitive mirror
> of a clear lake, so clear. . .
> so clear that sometimes I believe
> that on its crystalline page
> my thought is imprinted.
> Flower of air, flower of water,
> lake's soul is a swan
> with two human pupils, . . .
> Water I give him in my hands
> and he seems to drink fire;
> and I appear to offer him
> all the glass of my body. . .

When Delmira Augustini finally found her ideal love, her story ended tragically. After a brief two months of marriage, she was killed by her husband who then committed suicide.

Nearby, in Buenos Aires, Alfonsina Storni (1892-1938), disillusioned with love, cynical about men and society, committed suicide by walking into the sea rather than face her final illness. Storni had written a large amount of verse, much of it marred by extreme didacticism. At its best, however, her verse is fresh, spontaneous, direct:

> I don't ask you to tell me the great truths
> Because you wouldn't tell me; I only ask
> If, when you carried me in your belly, strolling through
> Dark patios in bloom, the moon was a witness.

Alfonsina Storni lived an unusual life for a woman of her day, giving birth to an illegitimate baby that she reared on her own, supporting him by a series of jobs—as cashier, clerk, secretary. She began to write articles for newspapers and magazines as her work gained increasing recognition.

Not only her life, but her poems, expressed her rebellion. She could write such feminist poems as "You Want Me to Be White," a poem which expresses her bitterness about the double standard and which tells men what they must do before they can demand chastity of women ("Run away to the woods, . . ./ Sleep on the white frost./ Talk to the birds. . . ."). She could also address the pain of men and the "venom" a rare male tear held as a result of the macho ideal.

> You said to me: My father didn't cry;
> You said to me: My grandfather didn't cry;
> The men of my race have never cried,
> They were men of steel.

And she felt deeply the growing alienation brought on by the social changes in the early decades of the twentieth century—suburban houses so tiny, so identical, and so soul-diminishing that their inhabitants had square souls. Against this deadness, she poised her aliveness and passion.

> From mouth to mouth, over rooftops
> this cry went rolling:
> "Throw stones at her, right in her face!
> She's given her heart."

Eventually she was invited to speak in Chile with Gabriela Mistral and Juana de Ibarbourou, and she wrote about the poetry of Delmira Augustini. Sadly for her, as her work matured, the critics found it more and more difficult, more and more obscure. The two final books that she wrote were heavily influenced by French symbolism as she felt the impact of the ferment and struggle to create a poetry that expressed the twentieth century. However, Storni found the critical rejection of her work extremely painful, and she responded by becoming less social and more paranoid. She had her own circle of friends and her son, but they were not enough to protect her from the depression that she experienced during the early 1930's. In 1935, it was discovered that she had cancer and she underwent an operation. However, she was not cured, and when the cancer returned, she refused further treatment.

Chilean Gabriela Mistral (1889-1953), winner of the 1945 Nobel Prize for Literature, is the Latin American women poet best known in this country. Even so, the body of her work still remains to be translated, and her poems in translation are only available in two editions of selected poems. Mistral took the conventional themes of motherhood, love of children, and nature, and made of them something fresh, subtle, ardent, and somber. She does not fall into the trap of sentimentality, nor are the emotions she conveys simplistic. Her poems are spare, crisp, and painful:

OLD WOMAN

She is one hundred and twenty years old, one twenty,
and she's more wrinkled than Earth.
She wears so many wrinkles that she wears
nothing but tucks and tucks like the poor mat.

So many wrinkles as are made by the wind on the dune,
and it's the wind that powders her with dust and creases her;
so many wrinkles she shows that we look only
at her poor eternal carp scales. . . .

Her religious poems are direct, passionate, and never doctrinaire:

INTERROGATIONS

How, Lord, do the suicides remain sleeping?
A curdling in the mouth, the two breasts emptied,
the moons of the eyes white and swollen,
the hands set toward an invisible anchor?

Disappointed in an early love, Mistral never married or had the children she so much desired. Instead, she became a teacher, devoting herself to innovative approaches to teaching the young. Her pedagogical ideas were soon acclaimed and she was invited to speak all over Chile and in other countries. At the same time, her poems went on appearing in magazines and in books. But in spite of her importance and her originality, much of her work has never been translated into English and may never be. A new book of her poems with original translations by Doris Dana will be published in 1984 by The Latin American Literary Review Press.

Uruguay's Juana de Ibarbourou (1895-1977) was named "Juana de America" in 1929 by her country's government because of the popularity of her poetry and the purity of her song. Her first editor called her "Hebraic" and spoke of her "contagious pantheism" and "fragrant sensuality." A writer of prose as well as poetry, she contributed to newspapers and magazines and wrote two textbooks, two prose works and a book-length poem on religious subjects. Her poems were most frequently on properly "feminine" subjects:

nature and love. Her most distinctive qualities unfortunately never reached a full originality, but, instead, her spontaneity and freshness were muted by the veil of *modernismo.*

To a contemporary reader, her love poems seem tame,

> I grew
> For you
> Cut me. . .
>
> I flowed
> For you
> Drink me. . .,

but for the reader of her time, such verse was frank and direct for a woman. Her constant use of nature imagery, celebration of freedom and exuberance, pantheism and animism, led her style to be characterized as "primitive" and to be much imitated. However, as Juana de Ibarbourou aged, the themes of simple joy and wild love give way to themes of nostalgia for the past and her wild roots. Her work has clarity, simplicity, feeling, workmanship. Unluckily, these virtues have not been sufficient to give her a place in literary history. Indeed, Enrique Anderson Imbert has called her primitivism "an obstinate narcissism."

Most readers will have no trouble agreeing that Delmira Augustini, Alfonsina Storni, Gabriela Mistral, and Juana de Ibarbourou stand out as the great women poets of the earlier generation of Latin American poets. However, when we come to the generation of contemporaries, women born in this century, agreement becomes much more difficult to obtain. Although they are unknown or little known in the U.S., many women poets are now writing in Central and South America, so many that is difficult for a person here or in any single country of Latin America to have read them all! A few stand out because they have a large body of work which has been known and praised in Latin America or here by Hispanic scholars for several decades (e.g., Rosario Castellanos, Alejandra Pizarnik). Others have established reputations in their own coutries (Idea Vilariño, Ulalume González de León, Olga Orozco, Blanca Varela), but their work is not readily available elsewhere. Still others are exiles trying to work and publish in an adopted country (Uruguayan Ida Vitale in Mexico, Salvadorean Claribel Alegría in Spain, Peruvian Cecilia Bustamante and Cuban Rita Geada in the U.S.)

The question of the specific contributions of contemporary women poets to the larger world of poetry is difficult and problematic. If we measure Latin American women poets by their appearance in national and international anthologies, they have clearly been judged wanting—if, indeed, they have been judged at all since their work is frequently not even considered. To what degree is this their invisibility as women and to what degree their measurement against a false standard? Are there themes, kinds of imagery, language, particular to women poets generally or to Latin American women poets specifically?

Perhaps, but I am skeptical. Certainly, the nature of women's lives suggests certain themes for their poetry over and over again—the joys and restrictions of the domestic sphere, motherhood, the dimensions of relationships. But women poets are also concerned with themes common to contemporary poetry—the limits of language, the mysteriousness and threat of nature, the alienation of modern urban life, the plight of the poor and oppressed.

Latin American women's poems express the dialectics of modern poetry, pulling toward and then away from social poetry, toward and away from private poetry. At the same time, these women poets often must live in situations which control what they say, how they say it, and even prevent them from writing at all. Patriarchal societies, bolstered by the Catholic Church, prevent women from pursuing non-traditional roles and make it difficult for them to support themselves in jobs that will allow them the independence and the rooms of their own that they require. Even when they are rich, public and family pressure may militate against the concentration and single-mindedness necessary for literary achievement. Social class, in most countries of Latin America, remains an important obstacle too—free education is unavailable or, when available, not possible for a poor girl who must work to help her family. Another factor at work is the deliberate aloofness of Indian groups which, in preserving their own cultures, may prevent a woman poet from having an audience.

Generally speaking, there is no organized feminist movement in Latin America, although there are feminists (largely among women of the upper classes). Many women say that the economic, social, and political crises of their countries are so great that they must take precedence and that the problems women have are secondary and must wait.

Last, but not least, is the problem of political repression and how it shapes, controls, and limits the writing of women. It is certainly striking to look over the poetry of Latin American women and see how rare is the anguished outcry about the suffering of the poor, the plight of children, the torture of dissidents, the limitations imposed on women's lives. Instead, we have a retreat into poetry that may be skillfully written but which is oblique, symbolist or surrealist, other-worldly, distant from the tattered, dirty, and agonizing reality that is Latin America today.

Nonetheless, we can read the poems of Colombian María Merecedes Carranza and find, not the feminist complaining about the treatment of women or the radical criticizing her society, but the alienated and despairing modern woman—the speaker in these poems is the female counterpart to the Twentieth Century Man. We have the calm surfaces of the beautiful poems by Uruguayan Circe Maia below which lurk an ever-present but indefinable threat of a dangerous world, an icy terror of the uncontrollable. We have the exquisite poems of Mexican Ulalume González de León which show that modern concern of such male writers as Samuel Beckett and Octavio Paz with words and language as a determinant of reality. And no one has turned the techniques of Surrealism to more effective use than Alejandra Pizarnik of Argentina in her depiction of a world hallucinatory with pain.

Surely we have variety and richness and talent. If we add Mexican Rosario Castellanos with her feminist poems and Salvadorean Claribel Alegría with her social protest poems, we have a great range of theme, style, technique, voice. Finally, in no other country and in no other time have we had a more assertive and playful poem than María Sabina's Mazatec chant with its endless definition of Woman.

In order to increase knowledge of these poets and their work, a series of conferences have been arranged. Yvette Miller organized the First Congress of Latin American Women Writers at Carnegie-Mellon University in 1975 and a second meeting was held the following year at San Jose State College. These two meetings evolved into a biennial Conference on Inter-American women writers. At the Ottawa meeting in May 1978 and the Mexico City meeting in June 1981, women writers and scholars from the entire hemisphere had a chance to debate issues familiar to U.S. women poets—Is there a feminine voice? Do women write in a feminine tradition? They also discussed issues especially pertinent to Latin American women writers such as the challenge of providing education so that women of lower classes can write and so that all citizens can have the opportunity of reading poetry and the problem of dealing with social issues in poetry and trying to bring about change through literature of social protest. Latin American women poets had the chance to read their own poems and to hear them analyzed in critical essays and discussed by interested participants. They made contact with each other as well as with North American and Canadian women writers. Finally, they went home with the sense of the growing possibilities open to them and their work.

Today, many Latin American countries have dozens of strong women writers, virtually all of them unknown in this country. The average reader of poetry will still probably have heard only of Gabriela Mistral, winner of the 1945 Nobel Prize for Literature. And yet there are strong new generations of women poets in Mexico, in Uruguay, in Argentina, in Peru, in Chile, in Cuba, and brilliant individual poets in most of the other Latin American countries.

So, where in the U.S. can a reader find a Latin American woman writer either in her original Spanish or Portuguese or in translation? There are several anthologies that include a few poems by a few poets—*The Other*

Voice, The Penguin Book of Women Poets, and *Women Poets of the World*—and there are magazines available here which have encouraged Latin American women poets by publishing translations of their poems and sometimes the poems themselves. Recently poems by Latin American women poets have appeared in *American Poetry Review, Poetry Now, Webster Review, Colorado State Review,* and *Grove.* And Catherine Perricon has collected poems in Spanish for her anthology, *Alma y Corazón,* a book meant to be used in U.S. classrooms and which includes Sor Juana from the 17th century, the four poets from the 19th century discussed above, and 21 poets from the 20th century from 10 countries.

The present anthology follows Nora Wieser's *Open to the Sun* (Perivale Press, 1979), which begins earlier and contains a mostly different selection of poets. In addition, Brooklyn College has a two-volume anthology of Latin American women's writings under preparation. I hope that these books will be a beginning and that we will soon have available the work of many more Latin American women poets.

All of this means that, while all anthologies are arbitrary, this one must be more so. There are no doubt many fine poets whose work I have not even heard about. Certainly there are women I have heard about but whose work (or any quantity of it) I could not get. Finally, I had to choose poets and poems that would provide the reader as far as possible with the widest range of styles and themes.

For their help and encouragement, I would especially like to thank Ulalume González de León, the first woman poet I met in Latin America and who invited me to her Mexico City home and introduced me to Ida Vitale and her husband Enrique Fierro, who gave me names and addresses of women poets in Argentina and Uruguay. At that time, I also wrote to critics such as Raúl Aguirre in Buenos Aires and Saúl Yurkeivitch in Paris who kindly sent me lists of women poets to consider. In Bogotá, I met Anabel Torres who gave me her out-of-print copy of *Poesía de Autoras Colombianas* (Poetry of Colombian Women Writers), which led me to that country's women poets (whose work was otherwise impossible to obtain). In Buenos Aires, Monique and Carlos Altschul, translators of Ernesto Cardenal's *Homage to the American Indians,* with whom I'd been corresponding, treated me like a friend. They called poets for me, gave me names and addresses, introduced me to writers (as well as showing me the sights). In a brief visit to Montevideo, I was received cordially by a sick Nancy Bacelo, had a warm discussion over lunch with Amanda Berenguer and her family, and met Idea Vilariño in her library. By then I had too many books to carry and the U.S. Embassy shipped them all home for me! To all of these people, I want to express my gratitude and indebtedness.

So, gradually, I accumulated books and poems and names. Now I needed translators. Once back in the U.S., I sent more letters of inquiry—to the Center of Inter-American Relations in New York and to the Translation Center at the University of Texas, for example—trying to track down translators already at work on the poems of contemporary Latin American women poets. As it turned out, there were very few. But I found writers who wanted to work at this task and I sent manuscripts and addresses or they found works to translate on their own. While I was happy to be able to include the work of such distinguished and excellent translators as Eliot Weinberger and the late Donald Walsh, I felt strongly that in the task of introducing unknown but fine women poets to this country I ought also to try to introduce able but unknown women translators like Sara Nelson and Heather Sievert. Page by page, a book began to take shape.

Finally, in 1979, my search came to its end. With my list narrowed to 15 writers, I made the final choices and shaped a book that I believe will indeed demonstrate that Latin American women have shared in the literary boom. However, I could never have completed this work without the help of many other people. My choices represent the best translations of the best poems by the best poets that I could locate and also a balance among styles. Several excellent poets do not appear because I felt that I needed to include the fullest possible range of work and theirs, while excellent, was too similar to the work of women poets already included. Many people recommended to me women poets whose work I could not find in this country or through queries to translators or translation centers. This turned out to be one of the biggest problems. So, in many ways, this book represents a beginning, or many beginnings. Many other different kinds of collections should follow as well as books of translations of the poems of single poets.

My final thanks to all the translators who have helped and encouraged me, and my thanks especially to Patsy Boyer, my colleague and co-translator, who has made suggestions and intelligent recomendations throughout my task. My special thanks to Gregory Kolovakos, formerly of the Center for Inter-American Relations, who recommended a fundamental revision of my manuscript that led me to the final book. My final thanks to the Translation Center of Columbia University for a 1979 Translation Award that aided me in the completion of this manuscript and to Yvette Miller who obained a publication award from the National Edowment for the Arts for her non-profit press, which has made this anthology a reality at last.

MARY CROW

I am a woman wise in medicine, says
I bring my lord eagle, says
I bring my opossum, says
I bring my whirlwind of colors, says

I am a spirit woman, says
I am a woman of light, says
I am a woman of the day, says
I am a Book woman, says

I am a woman who looks into the insides of things, says
I am a whirling woman of colors, says
                                        María Sabina (Mexico)

Parts of an almost endless chant appear above; a longer passage is quoted at
the end as the final section by a woman poet. These chants are the oral poetry
of María Sabina, a Mazatec Indian woman, now in her eighties, whose voice
can be heard on a Folkways record. She is a medicine woman and sage who
belongs to a tribe that uses the hallucinogenic mushroom of her area near Oax-
aca in religious ceremonies, and she has the gift of inspiration when she eats
the mushroom ("says"). The chant has been recorded in Mazatec and
translated from Mazatec into Spanish by Eloína Estrada de González and
from Spanish into English by Henry Munn.

The title for this anthology came from her chant, and it is to her and her song
that I dedicate this book.

ALEJANDRA PIZARNIK was born in Buenos Aires in 1936 and was educated in the visual arts as well as literature. Before she committed suicide in 1972, she had published eight books of poems: *La tierra más ajena* (1955), *La última inocencia* (1956), *Las aventuras perdidas* (1958), *Arból de Diana* (1962), *Los trabajos y las noches* (1965), *Extracción de la piedra de locura* (1968), *Nombres y figuras* (1969), and *El infierno musical* (1971). She divided her time between Argentina and France where she was involved with various magazines, both Spanish and French, writing critical articles and translating French poetry into Spanish, but wherever she was she went on turning out her beautiful and painful poems. According to one critic, "There is in her poems a mixture of mocking and suffering, of dream and suffering, that comes perhaps from her preoccupation with fantastic literature." Pizarnik is known for her surrealist imagination which leaps without losing contact with the ordinary and the concrete. Before her death a friend wrote to her of her poems, "They are animals—pretty and a little cruel, a little neurasthenic and tender; they are the prettiest animals. . .they are little wild beasts covered with skin, perhaps a species of cinchilla; you have to give them blood in luxury and with caresses. I love your poems; I wish that you may create many and that your poems would spread love and terror everywhere."

Ojos primitivos

En donde el miedo no cuenta cuentos y poemas, no forma
figuras de terror y de gloria.

Vácio gris es mi nombre, mi pronombre.

Conozco la gama de los miedos y ese comenzar a cantar
despacito en el desfiladero que reconduce hacia mi desfiladero
que reconduce hacia mi desconocida que soy, mi emigrante de sí.

Escribo contra el miedo. Contra el viento con garras que se
aloja en mi respiración.

Y cuando por la mañana temes encontrarte muerta (y que no haya
más imágenes): el silencio de la comprensión, el silencio del mero
estar, en esto se van los años, en esto se fue la bella alegría
animal.

Infancia

Hora en que la yerba crece
en la memoria del caballo.
El viento pronuncia discursos ingenuos
en honor de las lilas,
y alguien entra en la muerte
con los ojos abiertos
como Alicia en el país de lo ya visto.

Primitive Eyes

Where fear doesn't tell stories and poems, doesn't form
figures of terror and glory.

Gray void is my name, my pronoun.

I recognize the gamut of fears and how beginning to sing very
slowly on the narrow ledge takes me once more to my unknown who I
am, my own emigrant.

I write against fear. Against the wind with claws that
lodges in my breath.

And when you fear in the morning that you'll find yourself
dead (and that there'll be no more images): silence of compression,
silence of mere being. In this, years escape; in this, beautiful
animal joy escaped.

(Translated by Susan Pensak)

Childhood

Hour in which the grass grows
in memory of the horse.
Wind delivers artless speeches
in honor of lilacs,
and someone enters death
with eyes open
like Alice in the land of *dêja vu*.

(Translated by Susan Pensak)

Del otro lado

Como un reloj de arena cae la
música en la música.

Estoy triste en la noche de colmi-
llas de lobo.

Cae la música en la música como
mi voz en mis voces.

En un ejemplar
de «Les chants de maldoror»

Debajo de mi vestido ardía un campo con flores
alegres como los niños de la medianoche.

El soplo de la luz en mis huesos cuando escribo la
palabra tierra. Palabra o presencia seguida por animales
perfumados; triste como sí misma, hermosa como el suicidio;
y que me sobrevuela como una dinastía de soles.

From The Other Side

Like sand in an hourglass
music falls over music.

I am sad on this wolf-fanged
night.

Music falls over music
as my voice over my voices.

(Translated by Lynne Alvarez)

From a Copy
of «Les chants de maldoror»

Beneath my dress a field of flowers,
bright as midnight children, burned.

The breath of light in my bones when I write the
word earth. Word of presence followed by perfumed
animals; sad as herself, lovely as suicide; and which
hovers over me like a dynasty of suns.

(Translated by Lynne Alvarez)

El entendimiento

Empecemos por decir que Sombra había muerto. ¿Sabía Sombra que Sombra había muerto? Indudablemente. Sombra y ella fueron consocias durante años. Sombra fue su única albacea, su única amiga y la única que vistió luto por Sombra. Sombra no estaba tan terriblemente afligida por el triste suceso y el día del entierro lo solemnizó con un banquete.

Sombra no borró el nombre de Sombra. La casa de comercio se conocía bajo la razón social "Sombra y Sombra". Algunas veces los clientes nuevos llamaban Sombra a Sombra; pero Sombra atendía por ambos nombres, como si ella, Sombra, fuese en efecto Sombra, quien había muerto.

The Understanding

We begin by saying Shadow had died. Did Shadow know that
Shadow had died? Undoubtedly. Shadow and she had been partners
for years. Shadow was her only executor, her only friend, the
only one who wore mourning for Shadow. Shadow wasn't so terribly
grieved by the sad event and the day of the burial she solemnized
it with a banquet.

Shadow did not erase Shadow's name. The firm was known
under the name of "Shadow and Shadow." Sometimes new clients
would call Shadow Shadow; but Shadow answered to both names, as
if she, Shadow, were in effect Shadow, who had died.

(Translated by Susan Pensak)

Exilio

Esta manía de saberme angel
sin edad
sin muerte en que vivirme
sin piedad por mi nombre
ni por mis huesos que lloran vagando.

¿Y quién no tiene un amor?
¿Y quién no goza entre amapolas?
¿Y quién no posee un fuego, una muerte,
un miedo, algo horrible,
aunque fuere con plumas,
aunque fuere con sonrisas?

Siniestro delirio amar a una sombra.
La sombra no muere.
Y mi amor
solo abraza a lo que fluye
como lava del infierno:
una logia callada,
fantasmas en dulce erección,
sacerdotes de espuma,
y sobre todo ángeles,
ángeles bellos como cuchillos
que se elevan en la noche
y desvastan la esperanza.

Exile

This mania to see myself as an angel,
ageless
without a death in which to live
without pity for my name
or for my bones which weep wandering.

And who doesn't have a love?
And who doesn't feel joy among the poppies?
And who doesn't possess a fire, a death,   .
a fear, something horrible
even if it's feathered
even if it comes with smiles?

Sinister delusion to love a shadow.
The shadow doesn't die.
And my love
only embraces what is fluid
as lava from hell:
a silent lodge
ghosts sweetly erect
priest of foam
and above all angels
angels as beautiful as knives
that rise up during the night
and lay waste to hope.

(Translated by Lynne Alvarez)

RENATA PALLOTTINI was born in São Paolo, Brazil, in 1937. She studied law and philosophy and took a position as a lawyer for two years. Later she turned to work in the theatre, and she currently teaches at the University Theatre in São Paolo. She has won several awards for both her poems and her plays (including an award from PEN, the Molière Prize from the French government, and an award for a TV play from the São Paolo Critics Association). Several of her plays have been performed in Brazil and abroad. Her books of poems began to appear in 1952 and her most recent one was published in 1980; they include *Acalanto, O Monólogo Vivo, A Casa, Livro de Sonetos, A Faca e a Pedra, Os Arcos da Memória, Noite Afora, Chão de Palavras, Coração Americano,* and *Cantar Meu Povo.* Her poems ring with pain, the sources of which are only hinted at. The world she sees is cruel but life can still give such small delights as «a loaf of bread and three grapes» and poems can carve truths in the night.

Naquela Noite

Naquela noite
forrei com jornal os sapatos de inverno
molhei as mãos no vinho
e saí contente para a rua antigua
com um pedaço de pão e três passas no bolso.

Brilhavam os cafés esfumaçados,
o amor encharcava as árvores vazias
e havia uma chuva de castanhas quentes
diante de cada taverna escondida.

Meu caminho passava ao lado de tudo o que é possível,
eu conquistava o velho mundo em barcos que voltavam,
a América era um sonho que ficara para trás.

Teu corpo era pequeno e vermelho
                                    e o teu riso —
jamais esquecerei o teu riso   —   ele se abria.

A noite estava ali, de passagem, como un bólido.
E eu tinha o defeito alegre de ser casta e jovem.

That Night

That night
I lined my winter shoes with paper
dipped my hands in wine
and left happy down the old road
with a loaf of bread and three grapes in my sack.

The smoky cafés shone
love drew pools around the empty trees
and there was a drizzle of warm chestnuts
before every hidden tavern.

My path led past everything you can imagine
I was conquering the old world in returning boats
America was a dream remaining behind.

Your body was small and red
                              and your laughter
I shall never forget your laughter   it opened.

the night was there, on its way, like a meteor.
And my happy flaws were youth and chastity.

(Tanslated by Monique and Carlos Altschul)

Mensagem

Conta ao teu filho, meu filho,
daquilo que nós passamos;
que havia fitas gravadas,
retratos de corpo inteiro.
Conta que nos encolhemos
como animais espancados;
que ninguém teve coragem,
que respirávamos baixo,
olhos fugindo dos olhos,
as mãos frias e suadas.
E conta que faz dez anos,
que temos pouca esperança,
que pedimos testemunho
e não aguentamos mais.
Talvez teu filho, meu filho,
viva en mundo mais aberto,
mas é grave
que lhe contes calmamente
e nos mínimos detalhes
a história desses punhais
cravados em nossas tardes.
Porém se por tudo isso
renuncias a ter filhos
como (alguns) renunciamos,
deixa inscritos como eu deixo
sinais em troncos de árvores,
letras em papéis esquivos
para que não escureça
esta lâmpada mesquinha,
relâmpago, fogo fátuo,
pura lembrança dos dias
em que livres fomos filhos
de pais muito mais felizes.
Conta a quem possas, meu filho;
o que em ti forem palavras
nos outros serão raízes.

Message

Tell your son, my son,
what we endured:
there were taped confessions
and pictures full face.
Tell how we shrunk
like beaten beasts;
that nobody had the courage,
that we breathed in shame,
eyes fleeing other eyes,
hands cold and sweating.
And tell how for ten years past
we have had
little hope:
we ask someone to bear witness
and we cannot take it any longer.
Maybe your son, my son,
will live in an open world,
but it is basic
you tell him calmly
and in minutest detail
the story of those daggers
stuck in our afternoons.
Yet if for this reason
you give up having sons
as some of us have
leave inscriptions as I do
signs on tree bark,
letters on elusive paper,
so this puny flare,
lightning, will o' the wisp,
will not go dark.
Pure memory of those days
in which we were free sons
of happier parents.
Tell whoever you can, my son.
What were words in you
will be roots in them.

(Translated by Monique and Carlos Altschul)

O Grito

Se ao menos esta dor servisse
se ela batesse nas paredes
abrisse portas
falasse
se ela cantasse e despenteasse os cabelos

se ao menos esta dor se visse
se ela saltasse fora da garganta como um grito
caísse da janela fizesse barulho
morresse

se a dor fosse um pedaço de pão duro
que a gente pudesse engulir com força
depois cuspir a salive fora
sujar a rua os carros o espaço o outro
esse outro escuro que passa indiferente
e que não sofre tem direito de não sofrer

se a dor fosse só a carne do dedo
que se esfrega na parede de pedra
para doer doer visível
doer penalizante
doer com lágrimas

se ao menos esta dor sangrasse

The Shriek

If at least this pain helped
if it knocked walls
if it opened doors
if it spoke
if it sang and uncombed my hair

if at least this pain saw itself
if it sprung from the throat like a shriek
if it fell from the window if it would burst
if it would die

if the pain were a piece of hard bread
one could swallow with strength
and spit out after
stain the street the cars the space the other
that dark other which passes indifferently
and does not suffer who has a right not to suffer

if pain were only finger flesh
which can be rubbed on stone wall
so it hurts hurts visibly
painfully
with tears

if at least this pain would bleed

(Translated by Monique and Carlos Altschul)

Escrever. . .

Escrever
palavras.
Pôr um traço de giz
na noite alta.
Pôr a lua
na tua
mata de faias, paisagem.
Escrever porque viva,
de passagem.
Recortar silhuetas
de palavras;
desenhar com as letras
coisas bravas
que não podem ser ditas
(nem pensadas).
Escrever
as chaves.
Só depois
ver o que abrem.

To Write. . .

To write
words.
To trace chalk
in the high night.
To place the moon
landscape
in your brush of beeches.
To write on my way
as I live.
To cut out profiles
of words;
to draw with letters
tough statements
that cannot be said
(nor thought).
To write
the keys.
Only later
find what they open.

(Translated by Monique and Carlos Altschul)

DELIA DOMINGUEZ was born in Osorno, Chile, in 1934, and most of her poetry is full of landscapes and imagery from her native province which is in the cold south of Chile. In 1954 she moved to Santiago and it was there that she began her literary career. She has published six books, *Simbólico retorno* (1955), *La tierra nace al canto* (1958), *Obertura siglo xx* (1961), *Parlamentos del hombre claro* (1963), *Contracanto* (1968), *El sol mira para atrás* (1977), and *Leche de mujer* (1982), a colloquial book based on the life of Southern Chile. In 1977, she became poetry editor of the magazine *Paula.* Her lyrics derive their vitality from the people and land of her native region and are striking in their simplicity and humanity. (Recently her family was forced, as a result of the economic crisis in Chile, to sell their ranch near Osorno, a place that had long been a source of inspiration for Domínguez.) Pablo Neruda, in his introduction to *El sol mira para atrás,* commented: "She knows how to walk without fear among thorns and stones, to wade torrents, to join animals, to unite herself with the chorus of austral birds without humbling herself before the tremendous natural power in order to converse with sadness and love with all objects and all beings." And he attributes his ability to "the tenderness she has acquired in understanding and defending her solitude." The final wish he has for Delia Domínguez is that the people who read her poems should love her as he loves her, that they should also be fed by "the substances infinitely fragrant that she brings us from so far away. Isn't this the destiny of bread and poetry?"

Los frascos azules

No sé la historia de mis frascos azules
pero crecí con ellos
con las lenguas del sol en sus contornos
y el relumbre
en la humedad salada de mis ojos.
Allí filtró la luz sus abanicos
cuando salimos de la infancia
y nos marcó la edad de golpe.

No sé la leyenda de los frascos,
una mano que amaba me los pasó en silencio:
eso fue todo. Alguien dijo una vez
que eran viajados, que tomaron el color del mar
cuando los colonos, hace ciento cincuenta años,
largaron sus velas en Hamburgo; que a lo mejor,
estaban en la vidriería del pueblo
cuando llegaron los primeros espejos
y los floreros transparentes,
o que salieron de la memoria de un anciano
que los fue trasladando
con sus tabaqueras y sus rifles
por las repisas blanqueadas de las casas
que se quedaron a morir en la lluvia.

En los frascos azules guardo el aire
que té daré algún día
cuando todo sea verdad.

The Blue Bottles

I don't know the story of my blue bottles
but I grew up with them
with the sun licking at their curves
and their lustre
in the salty dampness of my eyes.
There, light filtered its fans
when we went out from childhood
and were suddenly marked by age.

I don't know the legend of the bottles,
a loving hand passed them to me in silence:
that was all. Someone once told me
that they were well-traveled, that they took on the color of the sea
when the colonists, one hundred fifty years ago,
set sail from Hamburg; that probably
they were in the glassware shop of the town
when the first mirrors arrived
and the transparent vases,
or that they came from the memory of an old man
who gradually passed them,
with his tobacco pouches and rifles,
to the mantelpieces of the houses
that stayed behind to die in the rain.

In the blue bottles I keep the air
that I'll give you someday
when everything comes true.

(Translated by Marjorie Agosin)

El sol mira para atrás

En el cielo
el sol mira para atrás
porque tiene que llamar agua,
y tú conoces las señales
los sagrados olores de la tierra
y empiezas a lustrar tus botas
la escopeta del 16
que el abuelo colgó en el comedor
en ese otoño de su muerte.
Y en el morral huequeado por antiguos
        reventones de pólvora,
hay un juego de naipes gastados
como esa risa que fuimos perdiendo
cuando nos vendaron los sueños
para que creciéramos
más tranquilos, más ciegos,
y no preguntáramos
por qué el sol miraba para atrás
desde el umbral sonoro de la lluvia,
o por qué los que amábamos
no volvieron jamás
para justificar su eternidad
        a nuestro lado,
y tú
y yo
tuvimos que ir guardando las sillas vacías
pasando llave
en el óxido de la chapas antiguas
pasándonos una costura en la boca
para quedarnos
con las palabras estrictamente necesarias
a nuestro sencillo amor.
El sol mira para atrás
porque tiene que llamar agua
y se ilumina la copa de los manzanos
y nos entra un frío por las rodillas
avisándonos la primera señal.

The Sun Looks Back

In the sky
the sun looks back
because it must call for water,
and you know the signs
the sacred smells of the earth
and you begin to polish your boots
the 16-caliber shotgun
which grandfather hung in the dining room
in that autumn of his death.

And in the game bag pitted
        by ancient, powder blasts
there's a worn-out deck of cards
like that laughter we slowly lost
when they blindfolded our dreams
so we'd grow up
more tranquil, more unseeing
and so we wouldn't ask
why the sun looked back
from the sonorous threshold of the rain
or why those we loved
never again returned
to justify their eternity
        at our side;
and you
and I
had to begin putting away the empty chairs
turning the keys
in the rust of antique locks
stitching up our mouths
that we might retain only
the words strictly necessary
to our simple love.
The sun looks back
because it must call for water
and the crest of the apple trees glows faintly
and a chill creeps in through our knees
as a first sign of warning.

(Translated by Marjorie Agosin)

Adivino los sueños

Vendrán malas noticias
la leche se cortó antes de las 8,
yo soñé con aguas turbias, y las rodillas
me dolieron toda la santa noche.
Jaime mató el pitío anunciador
a la primera bala de su rifle
y no sé qué nieve de otro tiempo
se puso a blanquear el aire
y alguien dijo: 5 grados bajo cero
　se irán los afuerinos
　y quedaremos solos.

Hoy es sábado en el campo
y me acuerdo de otras cosas
avisadas por sueños:
　como la lombriz de perro
　la historia del pulmón
y esa muerte tuya en otro pueblo
cuando no pude llamarte
porque no había aprendido
todas las palabras.

I Read Fortunes in Dreams

Bad news will come:
the milk turned sour before 8,
I dreamed of troubled waters, and my knees
ached the whole blessed night.
Jaime killed the heralding birdsong
with the first bullet from his rifle
and I don't know what snow from other days
has set to whitening the air
and someone said: 5 degrees below zero.
    The outsiders will go away
    and we'll be left alone.

Today it's Saturday in the countryside
and I recall other things
warned of in dreams:
    like the dog-worm,
    the business about the lung
and that death of yours in another town
when I couldn't call you
because I hadn't learned
all the words.

(Translated by Marjorie Agosin)

VIOLETA PARRA was born in 1917 in San Carlos in Central Chile. She started to write songs at 12, and at 20 she was singing and acting in public, quickly finding an individual voice which spoke with passion of the suffering of ordinary people. Pablo Neruda, in a poem written years later, described her singing thus: "Ay, señora, what love abundantly/ gathered in the streets: you pulled songs out of the clouds of smoke,/ fire from the offering candles,/ . . .,/ you are rural as the little birds/ and at times you attack with lightning." After a period of living and singing in Valparaíso and Santiago, Violeta Parra began to travel and perform both in various parts of her own country and abroad. She was particularly interested in promoting Chilean folk music, an interest which culminated in the publication in France of *Poesía del Andes.* She also founded the Museum of Popular Arts in Concepción in the south of Chile and for a time directed it. During her thirties, she had begun to develop as a visual artist, painting and working as a ceramicist. In her forties, she wrote music for the movies and acted on TV. In 1964, she held the first exposition of an individual Latin American artist in the Louvre, showing her paintings, wire sculptures, and water colors. Her songs are available under a number of titles published in Spain and Latin America, including *Toda Violeta Parra, Violeta del Pueblo,* and *Décimas.* One of her songs, "Gracias a la vida," has been made popular in this country by Joan Baez. But in spite of her talents and her efforts in behalf of the poor, Violeta Parra did not feel satisfied with her own life. In 1967, she committed suicide.

Run-run se fue pa'l norte

En un carro de olvido,
antes del aclarar
de una estación del tiempo
decidido a rodar
Run-run se fué pa'l Norte
no sé cuando vendrá
vendrá para el cumpleaños
de nuestra soledad
a los tres días carta
con letras de coral
me dice que su viaje
se alarga más y más
se va de Antofagosta
sin dar una señal
y cuenta una aventura
que pasó a deletrear
ay ay ay de mí.

Al medio de un gentío
que tuvo que afrontar
un trasbordo por culpa
del último huracán
en un puerto quebrado
cerca de Vallenar
con una cruz al hombro
Run-run debió cruzar
Run-run se siguió su viaje
llegó al Tamarugal
sentado en una piedra
se puso a divagar
que sí que esto que el otro
que nunca que además
que la vida es mentira
que la muerte es verdad
ay ay ay de mí.

Run-Run Went North

In a cart of no memory
before the dawn
of a season of time
bound to turn
Run-run went north
I don't know when he'll come
he'll come for the birthday
of our solitude
after three days a letter
written in coral
says that his trip
gets longer and longer
he's leaving Antofagosta
with no word of warning
and tells a story
fully detailed
ay ay ay de mí.

A crucifix on his back
Run-run had to cross
a river in the midst
of a throng, forced
to transfer after
the last hurricane
in a broken-down port
near Vallenar
Run-run continued on
until Tamarugal, when
seated on a rock
he began to ramble
that yes, that this, that the other
that never, that furthermore
that life is a lie
that death is truth
ay ay ay de mí.

La cosa es que una alforja
se puso a trajinar
sacó papel y tinta
un recuerdo quizás
sin pena ni alegría
sin gloria ni piedad,
sin rabia ni amargura,
sin hiel ni libertad
vacía como el hueco
del mundo terreñal
Run-Run mandó su carta
por mandarla no más
Run-Run se fue pa'l Norte

yo me quedé en el Sur
al medio hay un abismo
sin música ni luz
ay ay ay de mí.

El calendario afloja
por las ruedas del tren
los números del año
sobre el filo del riel
más vueltas dan los fierros
más nubes en el mes
más largos son los rieles
más agrio es el después
Run-Run se fué pa'l Norte
que le vamos a hacer
así es la vida entonces
espinas de Israel
amor crucificado
corona del desdén
los clavos del martirio
el vinagre y la hiel
ay ay ay de mí.

He rummaged around
deep in his pouch
took out paper and ink
perhaps a remembrance
with no sadness or joy
no glory, or pity
no anger or bitterness
no rancor or freedom
empty as the hollow
of the earthly world
Run-run sent his letter
for the sake of sending it
Run-run went North
I stayed down South
in between an abyss
with no music or light
ay ay ay de mí.

On the wheels of the train
the calendar loosens
the numbers of the year
on the edge of the track
the more the irons turn round
the more clouds in the month
the longer the tracks
the more bitter the afterwards
Run-run went North
what can we do
so that's life then
thorns of Israel
crucified love
crown of scorn
nails of martyrdom
vinegar and gall
ay ay ay de mí.

(Translated by Bonnie Shepard)

Según el favor del viento

Según el favor del viento
va navegando el leñero,
atrás quedaron las rucas
para dentrar en el puerto;
corra Sur o corra Norte
la barquichuela gimiendo, llorando estoy,
según el favor del viento, me voy, me voy.

Del Norte viene el pellín
que colorea en cubierta,
habrán de venderlo en Castro
aunque la lluvia esté abierta,
o queme el sol de lo alto
como un infierno sin puerta, llorando estoy,
o la mar está revuelta, me voy, me voy.

En un rincón de la barca
está hirviendo la tetera,
a un lado pelando papas
las manos de alguna isleña,
será la madre del indio,
la hermana o la compañera, llorando estoy,
navegan lunas enteras, me voy, me voy.

Chupando su matecito
o bien su pescado seco,
acurrucado en su lancha
va meditando en su lancha
va meditando el isleño,
no sabe que hay otro mundo
de raso y de terciopelo, llorando estoy,
que se burla el invierno, me voy, me voy.

At the Mercy of the Wind

The woodman sails
at the mercy of the wind.
He left the huts behind
to enter the port;
sailing north or south,
the skiff shakes, I cry,
at the mercy of the wind,
I'm going, I'm going.

From the north comes redwood
reddening the decks.
They must sell it in Castro
though the rain pours down.
Either the sun burns on high,
a hell with no port, I cry,
or the sea storms,
I'm going, I'm going.

In a corner of the boat
the teapot is boiling,
the hands of some island woman
peel potatoes at one side,
maybe the Indian's mother,
his sister, or spouse. I cry,
for whole moons they sail,
I'm going, I'm going.

Sucking his cup of tea
or maybe his dried fish,
crouched in his skiff,
the island man ponders,
what does he know of the world
of satin and velvet, I cry,
the winter mocks,
I'm going, I'm going.

No es vida la del chilote,
no tiene letra ni pleito,
tamango llevan sus pies,
milcao y ají su cuerpo,
pellín para calentarse,
del frío de los gobiernos, llorando estoy,
que le quebrantan los huesos, me voy, me voy.

Despierte el hombre, despierte,
despierte por un momento,
despierte toda la patria
antes que se abran los cielos
y venga el trueno furioso
con el clarín de San Pedro, llorando estoy,
y barra los ministerios, me voy, me voy.

De negro van los chilotes
más que por fuera, por dentro,
con su plato de esperanza
y su frazada de cielo,
pidiéndole a la montaña
su pan amargo centeno, llorando estoy,
según el favor del viento, me voy, me voy.

Quisiera morir cantando
sobre de un barco leñero,
y cultivar en sus aguas
un libro más justiciero,
con letras de oro que diga
no hay padre para el isleño, llorando estoy,
ni viento pa su leñero, me voy, me voy.

This no life—the Chilote's—
no schooling, no courts,
ragged shoes for their feet,
potatoes and garlic to eat.
hard wood to keep warm
from the government's cold, I cry,
their bones are breaking,
I'm going, I'm going.

Wake up, people, wake up,
wake up for a moment,
wake up the whole country
before the skies open
and angry thunder comes
with St. Peter's trumpet I cry
and sweeps away the ministries,
I'm going, I'm going.

The Chilotes all in black
inside more than out
with their plate of hope
and their blanket of sky
begging the mountain
for their bitter bread, I cry,
at the mercy of the wind,
I'm going, I'm going.

I'd like to die singing
on a woodman's boat,
and grow in his waters
a book with more justice
and letters in gold saying
no father for the islander, I cry,
nor wind for the woodman,
I'm gong, I'm going.

(Translated by Bonnie Shepard)

Maldigo del alto cielo

Maldigo del alto cielo
las estrellas con su reflejo
maldigo los azulejos
destellos del arroyuelo
maldigo del bajo suelo
la piedra con su contorno
maldigo el fuego del horno
porque mi alma está de luto
maldigo los estatutos
del tiempo con sus bochornos
cuánto será mi dolor.

Maldigo la cordillera
de los Andes y de la Costa
maldigo Señor la angosta
y larga faja de tierra
también la paz y la guerra
lo franco y lo veleidoso
maldigo lo perfumoso
porque mi anhelo está muerto
maldigo todo lo cierto
y lo falso con lo dudoso
cuánto será mi dolor.

Maldigo la primavera
con sus jardines en flor
y del Otoño el color
yo lo maldigo de veras
a la nube pasajera
la maldigo tanto y tanto
porque me asiste un quebranto
maldigo el Invierno entero
con el Verano embustero
maldigo profano y Santo
cuánto será mi dolor.

Goddamn the Empty Sky

Goddamn the empty sky
and the stars at night
goddamn the ripply bright
stream as it goes by
goddamn the way stones lie
on dirt they're all the same
goddamn the oven's flame
because my heart is raw
goddamn the laws
of time in all their shame
my pain's as bad as that.

Goddamn the mountain chain
the coast range and the Andes
goddamnit Lord my land is
ten times as long as Spain
also crazy and sane
with candor and deceit
goddamn what smells so sweet
because my luck is out
goddamn what's not in doubt
what's messy and what's neat
my pain's as bad as that.

Goddamn the way the Spring
gets plants to blossom
and the colors of Autumn
goddamn the whole damn thing
clouds on the wing
goddamn them more and more
because I'm done for
goddamn Winter to bits
along with Summer's tricks
goddamn the saint the whore
my pain's as bad as that.

Maldigo a la solitaria
figura de la bandera
maldigo cualquier emblema
la Venus y la araucaria
el trino de la canaria
el cosmo y sus planetas
la tierra y todas sus grietas
porque me aqueja un pesar
maldigo del ancho mar
sus puertos y sus caletas
cuánto será mi dolor.

Maldigo luna y paisaje
los valles y los desiertos
maldigo muerto por muerto
y el vivo de rey a paje
el ave con su plumaje
y lo maldigo a porfía
las aulas y las sacristías
porque me aflije un dolor
maldigo el vocablo amor
con toda su porquería
cuánto será mi dolor.

Maldigo por fin lo blanco
lo negro con lo amarillo
obispos y monaguillos
ministros y predicandos
yo los maldigo llorando
lo libre y lo prisionero
lo dulce y lo pendenciero
le pongo mi maldición
en griego y en español
por culpa de un traicionero
cuánto será mi dolor.

Goddamn getting on your feet
to watch the flag go by
damn every kind of lie
Venus and Main Street
and the canary's tweet
the planets and their motions
the earth with its erosions
because my heart is sore
goddamn the ports and shores
of the enormous oceans
my pain's as bad as that.

Goddamn the moon and weather
desert and river bed   .
goddamn the dead the dead
and the living together
the bird with all its feathers
is such a goddamn mess
schools and places to confess
I'll tell you what I'm sick of
goddamn that one word love
with all its nastiness
my pain's as bad as that.

So goddamn the number eight
eleven nine and four
choir boys and monsignors
preachers and men of state
goddamn them it's too late
free man and prisoner
soft voice and quarreler
I damn them every week
in Spanish and in Greek
thanks to a two-timer
my pain's as bad as that.

(Translated by John Felstiner)

MARIA MERCEDES CARRANZA was born in Bogota, Colombia, in 1945, and studied philosophy and letters at the University of the Andes. Her work has appeared widely in magazines and anthologies (including *Nueva poesía colombiana, Antología crítica de la poesía colombiana, Poesía de autoras colombianas.* Her poems were first collected into *Vainas y otros poemas* (1972). She says: "Poetry today, in order to succeed, ought to enter the kitchen, drink Coca-Cola, take a jet, read Little Lulu, listen to the Beatles, . . . speak with Perez who waits at the bustop on the corner of 7th Street with his newspaper tucked under his arm, help Camilo Torres to shoot, ... We need a poetry that helps us to live . . . ," The critic Andrés Holgún has said that her poems "constitute an excellent antidote against sentimental excesses, transcendental themes, lyrical vagueness, and other venoms of our literature." In her new book of poems, *Tengo miedo: Poesia, 1976-1982*, she writes, "Afraid of what? Of everything: from a sleeve on the mantel, to fear itself, fear of fear." But she also wonders why, after all he has found, Ulysses ever wanted to return to Ithaca.

De boyaca en los campos

Allí, sentado, de pie,
a caballo, en bronce, en mármol,
llovido por las gracias de las palomas
y llovido también por la lluvia,
en cada pueblo, en toda plaza,
cabildo y alcaldía estás tú.
Marchas militares con coroneles
que llevan y traen flores.
Discursos, poemas,
y en tus retratos el porte de un general
que más que charreteras
lucía un callo en cada nalga
de tanto cabalgar por estas tierras,
y más que un físico a lo galán de Hollywood
tenía el ademán mestizo de una batalla perdida.
Centenarios de tu primer diente y de tu última sonrisa.
Cofradías de damas adoradoras
y hasta guerras estallan
por disputarse un gesto tuyo.
Los niños te imitan
con el caballo de madera y la espada de mentira.
Te han llenado la boca de paja, Simón,
te han vuelto estatua,
medalla, estampilla
y hasta billete de banco.
Porque no todos los ríos van a dar a la mar,
algunos terminan en las academias,
en los pergaminos, en los marcos dorados:
lo que también es el morir.
Pero y si de pronto, y si quizás, y si a lo mejor,
Y si acaso, y si tal vez algún día te sacudes la lluvia,
los laureles y tanto polvo, quién quita.

From Boyaca in the Country

There, seated, on foot,
on horseback, in bronze, in marble,
rained on by the antics of the pigeons
and also by the rain,
there you are in each town,
in every plaza, church and state.
Military marches with colonels
who come bearing flowers, speeches, poems.
And in your portraits the nobility of a general
bearing more than epaulets—
a callus on each buttock
from so much riding over this terrain,
and more than a Hollywood physique
the half-breed look of a lost battle.
Centennials of your first tooth and final smile,
sisterhoods of worshipful ladies,
and even wars break out
to commission one of your likenesses.
Children imitate you with wooden horse and false sword.
They have stuffed your mouth with straw, Simon,
they have turned you into a statue,
medal, stamp,
and even a bank-note.
Because not all rivers run to the sea,
some end in the academies,
on the parchement, in the gilded frames:
that also is death.
But if suddenly, maybe, and unexpectedly,
and if by chance, if perhaps someday you shake off
the rain, the laurels, and so much dust,
who can say.

(Translated by Ellen Watson)

Erase una mujer a una virtud pegada

"No tenía ganas de nada, sólo de vivir."
—*Juan Rulfo*

Yace para siempre
pisoteada,
cubierta de vergüenza,
muerta
y en nada convertida,
mi última virtud.
Ahora soy una mujer
de vida alegre,
una perdida: cumplo
con todos mis deberes,
soy pozo
de bondades, respiro
santidad
por cada poro.
Interrumpo la luz,
le cierro
la boca al viento,
borro las montañas,
tacho el sol,
el cero me lo como
y enmudezco el qué.
Elimino la vida.

Once Upon a Time a Woman Tied to a Virtue

"I had no desire for anything, only to live."
—Juan Rulfo

There it lies forever
trampled,
covered with shame,
dead
and converted into nothing—
my last virtue.
Now I am a woman
of easy virtue,
a woman lost: I perform
all my duties,
I am a well
of kindness, I breathe
holiness
from every pore.
I interrupt the light,
I close
my mouth to the wind,
I rub out the mountains,
erase the sun,
eat up the cipher,
and I silence the what.
I eliminate life.

(Translated by Mary Crow)

Patas arriba con la vida

"Sé que voy a morir porque no amo ya nada."
—*Manuel Machado*

Moriré mortal,
es decir habiendo pasado
por este mundo
sin romperlo ni mancharlo.
No inventé ningún vicio,
pero gocé de todas las virtudes:
arrendé mi alma
a la hipocresía: he traficado
con las palabras,
con los gestos, con el silencio;
cedí a la mentira:
he esperado la esperanza,
he amado el amor,
y hasta algún día pronuncié
la palabra Patria;
acepté el engaño:
he sido madre, ciudadana,
hija de familia, amiga,
compañera, amante.
Creí en la verdad:
dos y dos son cuatro,
María Mercedes debe nacer,
crecer, reproducirse y morir
y en esas estoy.
Soy un dechado de siglo XX.
y cuando el miedo llega
me voy a ver televisión
para dialogar con mis mentiras.

Heels Over Head with Life

"I know I'm going to die because I no longer love anything."
—Manuel Machado

I will die mortal,
that is to say having passed
through this world
without breaking or staining it.
I didn't invent a single vice,
but I tasted all the virtues:
I leased my soul
to hypocrisy: I have trafficked
with words,
with signs, with silence;
I surrendered to the lie:
I have hoped for hope,
I have loved love,
and one day I even pronounced
the words My Country;
I accepted the hoax:
I have been mother, citizen,
daughter, friend,
companion, lover;
I believed in the truth:
two and two are four,
María Mercedes ought to be born,
ought to grow, reproduce herself and die
and that's what I'm doing.
I am the sampler of the 20th century.
And when fear arrives
I go to watch television
in order to dialogue with my lies.

(Translated by Mary Crow)

RITA GEADA was born in Pinar del Río City, Cuba, on September 7, 1937, and was educated at the University of Havana. She taught for two years at the University of Buenos Aires, Argentina, and now teaches at Southern Connecticut State College in New Haven. Her five books are *Desvelado Silencio, Pulsar del Alba, Cuando Cantan las Pisadas, Mascarada,* and *Vertizonte. Mascarada* won the "Carabela de Oro" Prize from Spain in 1969. Geada's work has also been widely published in magazines here and abroad and has been translated into English, Italian, Portuguese, and French. In *La Literatura Cubana,* Raimundo Lazo said of her, "Rita Geada stands out in the Post-Revolutionary Cuban generation of poets for the felicitous expression of her introspective and anguished poetry." Over and over again she notes in her poems the dehumanization of contemporary life and the loss of power of language. But she does so without self-pity, in words carefully chosen to help bring back the efficacy of words. Her style is terse, elliptical, clean.

Para que ardan

Para que ardan todas las mentiras del mundo
he de arder.
Para que las llamas se destruyan a sí mismas
has de arder.
Falta un tramo.
Sólo un tramo.
Saltando.
Alcanzándolo podemos ver
el esqueleto
de todas las mentiras del mundo.

Devolvedme mi mundo

Devolvedme mi mundo
con sus ángeles de luz y de tinieblas.
Pero no estos cadáveres.
Estas garras.
Estas estatuas en venta alineadas.
Siempre iguales.
¡Ya gastadas!
El péndulo las mide y las domina.
Nada traen del arco-iris fugado entre los dedos.
Enfrentadme a otras miradas.
A otras manos.
A otros gestos.
A otras palabras.
Ahora que todo se va volviendo negro,
negro,
negro.
¿Donde están los colores, sus matices?
Devolvedme lo mío o aunque sea
pedazos de su luz deshilachada.

So That They Will Burn

So that all the world's lies will burn
I must burn.
So that the flames will destroy themselves
you must burn.
A span is missing
Only a single span.
Leaping.
Reaching it we can see
the skeleton
of all the lies in the world.

(Translated by Donald D. Walsh)

Give me Back my World

Give me back my world
with its angels of light and darkness.
But not these corpses.
These claws.
These statues lined up for sale.
Always the same.
Already out of date!
The clock measures them and controls them.
They bring nothing of the rainbow fled between the fingers.
Confront me with other looks.
With other hands.
With other gestures.
With other words.
Now that everything is slowly turning black,
black,
black.
Where are the colors, their shades?
Give me back what is mine even though it's only
pieces of its threadbare light.

(Translated by Donald D. Walsh)

En el aquelarre

¡Venir a mí con esas historias!
Hablarme de credos y de revoluciones y de guerrillas
y de crímenes y de feudalismos y de justicia social.
Nada menos que a mí
tanto tiempo suspendida entre la vida y la muerte.
Sangrante.
Hambrienta.
Exhausta.
A mí en holocausto. Antorcha viva en la plaza de Wenceslao.
A mí pasto de buitres
oyendo siempre el aullido de los lobos,
presenciando el asalto de tigres hambrientos de vísceras humanas,
insatisfechos siempre.
¡Venir a mí con esos cuentos dorados!
¡Feliz, feliz entretenimiento!
Vosotros que sólo ponéis la boca y la lengua
y los dientes si la ocasión es propicia.
Con esos cuentos a mí que como Tántalo respiro,
desgarrados los poros,
sintiendo caer la gota, la gota inmensa, intermitente.
Devorada por tenebrosos túneles,
de días, noches, meses, años, siglos.
En el aquelarre.
En su médula. Claveteada.
Oliendo hasta el hueso el zumo de lo cierto,
su humo. La verdad de lo increíble.
Lo increíble de la realidad.
La realidad tal cual, sin engaños, sin afeites,
desnuda, en su llaga.
El infierno sin disfraces de palabras.
Venir a mí, ¡nada menos que a mí!
empuñando tridentes de palabras
en el espantoso mercado,
en el delicioso,
en el continuo festín
de nuestra época.

On the Witches' Sabbath

To come to me with those stories!
To talk to me of creeds and revolutions and guerrilla bands
and crimes and feudalism and social justice!
To me no less
so long suspended between life and death.
Bloodied.
Starving.
Exhausted.
To me as a burnt offering. A living torch in Wenceslaus Square.
To me food for vultures
always hearing the howling of the wolves,
witnessing the assault of hungry tigers on human entrails,
always insatiate.
To come to me with those gilded tales!
Happy, happy entertainment!
You who offer your mouths and tongues
and teeth only if the occasion is propitious.
With those tales to me who breathe like Tantalus,
my flesh torn,
feeling the drop fall, the immense, the intermittent drop.
Devoured by dismal tunnels,
of days, nights, months, years, centuries.
On the Witches' Sabbath.
In its marrow. Nailed.
Smelling to the bone the justice of what is certain,
its smoke. The Truth of the incredible.
The incredible side of reality.
Reality just as it is, without deceits, without make-up,
naked, in its wound.
Hell, with no word disguises.
To come to me, no less!
clutching tridents of words
in the fright-filled market,
in the delightful,
in the endless banquet
of our time

(Translated by Donald D. Walsh)

Cuban NANCY MOREJON was born in Havana in 1944 and still lives there, working at the Cuban Union of Writers and Artists and writing about the city. Trained in French language and literature at the University of Havana, she has translated French poetry and is also an expert on the work of Cuban poet Nicolás Guillén. Her books of poetry are: *Mutismos* (1962), *Amor, ciudad atribuida* (1964), *Richard traja su flauta y Otros argumentos* (1967), *Piedra Pulida* (1974), *Parajes de una época* (1979), and *Octubre imprescindible* (1983). In addition, she has written a study of miners from the district of Nicaro, *Lengua de Pájaro*, in collaboration with Carmen Gonce, which appeared in 1969. "My womanhood is reflected in my poetry," according to Morejón, "but I wouldn't go so far as to call it a style. I think my class origin influences and determines my vision of many phenomena, not only poetry, but culture in general. No vital experience can be foreign to a human being no matter what her profession. That's why I don't believe that women's poetry or a woman's novel as such exists. A woman might not write like another woman but much more like the great men writers who have existed. Literature, art, poetry, are gifts, and also crafts, requiring in the first place the condition of being human." In the spring of 1983, Morejón toured the U.S. for the writer's exchange program of the Center for Cuban Studies. While here, she spoke at Columbia, Yale, Amherst, Johns Hopkins, Smith, and the University of California. *Black Scholar* sponsored her West Coast tour.

A un muchacho

Entre la espuma y la marea
se levanta su espalda
cuando a tarde ya
iba cayendo sola.

Tuve sus ojos negros, como hierbas,
entre las conchas brunas del Pacífico.

Tuve sus labios finos
como una sal hervida en las arenas.

Tuve, en fin, su barbilla de incienso
bajo el sol.

Un muchacho del mundo sobre mi
y los cantares de la Biblia
modelaron sus piernas, sus tobillos
y las uvas del sexo
y los himnos pluviales que nacen de su boca
envolviendonos si como a dos nautas
enlazados al velamen incierto del amor.

Entre sus brazos, vivo.
Entre sus brazos duros quise morir
como un ave mojada.

To a Boy

Between foam and tide
his back rises up
when the afternoon
was already sinking unaided.

I had his black eyes, like weeds,
between the damson shells of the Pacific.

I had his thin lips
like a salt boiled in the sands.

I had, finally, the incense of his beard
beneath the sun.

A boy of the world over me
and the songs of the Bible
shaped his legs, his ankles
and the grapes of his sex
and the pluvial hymns born of his mouth
enveloping us as if two mariners
lashed to the uncertain sails of love.

Between his arms, I live.
Between his strong arms I wanted to die
like a wet bird.

(Translated by Heather Sievert)

Nancy Morejón

hay el calor de piedra y cristal blando
que humedece esta tierra
el laberinto de saludos

hay la perenne acusación de los afables barrios
            modestos
el humo del edificio aledaño quema como si él
            mismo
encendiese un gastado farol de corazón y carne
hay naturaleza y estaciones
hay a pesar nuestro melancolía un poco de costumbre

hay la atención al trabajo ruidoso
hay la elegancia infantil
            los cines están llenos
hay color de gentes abrazándose a gente
hay el calor oscuro y corpulente

Nancy Morejón

there is the warmth of stone and soft crystal
that moistens this earth
the labyrinth of greetings

there is the perpetual accusation of the friendly
          modest neighborhood
the smoke of the nearby building burns as if it
might light up a burned out streetlight of
          heart and flesh
there is nature and seasons
there is to our regret somewhat customary sadness
there is the attention to noisy work
there is the childish elegance
          the movie theatres full
there is color of people embracing each other
there is warmth dark and fat

(Translated by Heather Sievert)

Masacre

El agua de la fronda
cae en los infiernos plenos del gorilla.

Cejas de tucán y cangrejo.
Bolas de maíz para la hacienda.

Miras la lluvia parda
y el saco roto del poeta
corre en el agua de los charcos limeños.

¿Qué tiempo vive Arauca
sentada a la puerta de todas las eras?

Trenza invisible de las venas
por donde cruzan cóndores y palmares
y la sombra perenne de la daga
vertida sobre nocturnas vísceras del océano.
Los rios fungiendo como dioses acuáticos.
El follaje trinando en Pernambuco.
El hungán clamando al pie del viento.

—Qué simple, *Madame,* fuera
traducir grito por masacre.

Massacre

The water from the leaf
falls on the full hells of the gorilla.

Narrow paths of toucan and crab.
Seeds of corn for the farm.

Look at the brown rain
and the torn jacket of the poet
running in the water of the ponds of Lima.

How long does Arauca live
seated in the doorway of time?

Invisible braid of the veins
through which condors and palm trees cross
and the perennial shadow of the dagger
spilled over the visceral night of the ocean.
The rivers swelling like water gods.
The foliage becoming angry in Pernambuco.
The Shaman imploring at the foot of the wind.

How simple, Madam, it would be
to translate shout for massacre.

(Translated by Heather Sievert)

ROSARIO CASTELLANOS, born in Chiapas in 1925, died as the result of an accident in Tel Aviv in 1974, where she was living as Mexican ambassador to Israel. In the years between, she worked at a variety of jobs and produced a range of writing. For some years she taught at the National University and contributed to the newspaper *Excelsior*. Her writing included two novels, three collections of short stories, four volumes of essays and criticism, several plays, and a dozen books of poems. Her poetry shows a marked social concern, and in it she explores, describes, and works against the many varieties of domination around her—of men over women, of whites over Indians, of North Americans and Europeans over Mexicans, of the upper classes over the lower classes, of parents over children. But she realized that change was going to be slow and she said, "And the laugh, now we know it, is the first testimonial of liberty." The strong feminism of many of her poems is unusual in Latin American women's poetry, and she frequently makes effective use of the dramatic monologue to express woman's anger, pain, bitterness, and compassion. Her language is direct and conversational, spare and telling. Her many books of poems include: *Trayectoria del polvo* (1948), *De la vigilia estéril* (1950), *Presentatión en el templo* (1952), *Apuntes para una declaración de fe* (1953), *Al pie de la letra (1959), and Lívida luz* (1960). Her poems have been collected under the title, *Poesía no eres tú. Looking at the Mona Lisa* is the title of a chapbook of translations of Castellanos' poems that Maureen Ahern published in 1981 in England.

Silencio cerca de una piedra antigua

Estoy aquí, sentada, con todas mis palabras
como con una cesta de fruta verde, intactas.

Los fragmentos
de mil dioses antiguos derribados
se buscan por mi sangre, se aprisionan, queriendo
recomponer su estatua.
De las bocas destruidas
quiere subir hasta mi boca un canto,
un olor de resinas quemadas, algún gesto
de misteriosa roca trabajada.
Pero soy el olvido, la traición,
el caracol que no guardó del mar
ni el eco de la más pequeña ola.
Y no miro los templos sumergidos;
sólo miro los árboles que encima de las ruinas
mueven su vasta sombra, muerden con dientes ácidos
el viento cuando pasa.
Y los signos se cierran bajo mis ojos como
la flor bajo los dedos torpísimos de un ciego.
Pero yo sé: detrás
de mi cuerpo otro cuerpo se agazapa,
y alrededor de mí muchas respiraciones
cruzan furtivamente
como los animales nocturnos en la selva.
Yo sé, en algún lugar,
lo mismo
que en el desierto el cactus,
un constelado corazón de espinas
está aguardando un nombre como el cactus la lluvia.
Pero yo no conozco más que ciertas palabras
en el idioma o lápida
bajo el que sepultaron vivo a mi antepasado.

Silence Near an Ancient Stone

I'm sitting here with all my words intact
like a basket of green fruit.

The fragments
of a thousand ancient and defeated gods
seek and bind each other in my blood, straining
to rebuild their statue.
From their shattered mouths
a song struggles to rise to mine,
an aroma of burnt resin, some gesture
of mysterious carved stone.
But I am oblivion, betrayal,
the shell that did not hold an echo
from even the smallest wave in the sea.
I do not watch the submerged temples;
I watch only the trees moving their vast shadows
over the ruins, biting the passing wind
with acid teeth.
And the signs close beneath my eyes like
a flower under the awkward fingers of the blind.
Yet I know: behind
my body another body crouches,
and around me many breaths
cross furtively
like nocturnal animals in the jungle.
I know that in some place
the same
as the cactus in the desert,
a clustered heart of thorns, awaits a name
as the cactus does the rain.
But I know only as few words
in the language or the stone
beneath which they buried my ancestor alive.

(Translated by Maureen Ahern)

La casa vacía

Yo recuerdo una casa que he dejado.
Ahora está vacía.
Las cortinas se mecen con el viento,
golpean las maderas tercamente
contra los muros viejos.
En el jardín, donde la hierba empieza
a derramar su imperio,
en las salas de muebles enfundados,
en espejos desiertos
camina, se desliza la soledad calzada
de silencioso y blando terciopelo.

Aquí donde su pie marca la huella,
en este corredor profundo y apagado
crecía una muchacha, levantaba
su cuerpo de ciprés esbelto y triste.

(A su espalda crecían sus dos trenzas
igual que dos gemelos ángeles de la guarda.
Sus manos nunca hicieron otra cosa
más que cerrar ventanas.)

Adolescencia gris con vocación de sombra,
con destino de muerte:
las escaleras duermen, se derrumba
la casa que no supo detenerte.

Empty House

I remember a house I left behind.
It's empty now.
Curtains blowing in the wind,
boards clapping stubbornly
against old walls.
In the garden where grass begins
to spill its borders,
through the rooms of covered furniture,
among the empty mirrors,
loneliness
glides and wanders
on silent velvet feet.

A girl grew up here,
her slim sad cypress body sprouted
where her footsteps have left their imprint
along the hollow silent corridor.

(Two braids stretching down her back
like twin guardian angels.
Her hands only knew how to
close windows.)

Grey adolescence, shadowy vocation,
a destiny of death:
the stairways sleep. A house
that could never hold you, collapses.

(Translated by Maureen Ahern)

Malinche

Desde el sillón del mando mi madre dijo: "Ha muerto."
Y se dejó caer, como abatida,
en los brazos del otro, usurpador, padrastro
que la sostuvo no con el respeto
que el siervo da a la majestad de reina
sino con ese abajamiento mutuo
en que se humillan ambos, los amantes, los cómplices.

Desde la Plaza de los Intercambios
mi madre anunció: "Ha muerto."

La balanza
se sostuvo un instante sin moverse
y el grano de cacao quedó quieto en el arca
y el sol permanecía en la mitad del cielo
como aguardando un signo
que fue, cuando partió como una flecha,
el ay agudo de las plañideras.

"Se deshojó la flor de muchos pétalos,
se evaporó el perfume,
se consumió la llama de la antorcha.

Una niña regresa, escarbando, al lugar
en el que la partera depositó su ombligo.

Regresa al Sitio de los que Vivieron.

Reconoce a su padre asesinado,
ay, ay, ay, con veneno, con puñal,
con trampa ante sus pies, con lazo de horca.

Se toman de la mano y caminan, caminan
perdiéndose en la niebla."

Malinche

From the throne of command my mother said: "He is dead."
And threw herself
into the arms of another, usurper, stepfather
who didn't sustain her with the respect
a servant renders to the majesty of a queen
but groveled in their mutual shame
of lovers and accomplices.

From the Plaza of Enchange
my mother announced: "She is dead."

The scale
balanced for an instant
the chocolate bean lay motionless in the bin
the sun remained at mid-point in the sky
waiting the sign
which shot like an arrow
became the sharp wail of the mourners.

"The bloom of many petals was deflowered,
the perfume evaporated,
the torch flame burned out.

A girl returns to scratch up the earth
in the place
where the midwife buried her umbilicus.

She returns to the Place of Those Who Once Lived.

She recognizes her father assassinated,
ay, ay, ay, poison, a dagger,
a snare before his feet, a vine noose.

They take each other by the hand and walk, walk
disappearing into the fog."

Tal era el llanto y las lamentaciones
sobre algún cuerpo anónimo; un cadáver
que no era el mío porque yo, vendida
a mercaderes, iba como esclava,
como nadie, al destierro.

Arrojada, expulsada
del reino, del palacio y de la entraña tibia
de la que me dió a luz en tálamo legítimo
y que me aborreció porque yo era su igual
en figura y en rango
y se contempló en mí y odió su imagen
y destrozó el espejo contra el suelo.

Yo avanzo hacia el destino entre cadenas
y dejo atrás lo que todavía escucho:
los fúnebres rumores con los que se me entierra.

Y la voz de mi madre con lágrimas ¡con lágrimas!
que decreta mi muerte.

Such were the wail and the lamentations
over an anonymous body: a corpse
that was not mine because I, sold
to the merchants, was on my way as a slave,
a nobody, into exile.

Cast out, expelled
from the kingdom, from the palace and from the warm belly
of her who bore me in legitimate marriage bed
who hated me because I was her equal
in stature and in rank
who saw herself in me and hating her image
dashed the mirror against the ground.

I advance toward destiny in chains
leaving behind all that I can still hear,
the funeral murmurs with which I am buried.

And the voice of my mother in tears—in tears!
she who decrees my death!

(Translated by Maureen Ahern)

Economía doméstica

He aquí la regla de oro, el secreto del orden:
tener un sitio para cada cosa
y tener
cada cosa en su sitio. Así arreglé mi casa.

Impecable anaquel el de los libros:
un apartado para las novelas,
otro para el ensayo
y la poesía en todo lo demás.

Si abres una alacena huele a espliego
y no confundirás los manteles de lino
con los que se usan cotidianamente.

Y hay también la vajilla de la gran ocasión
y la otra que se usa, se rompe, se repone
y nunca está completa.

La ropa en su cajón correspondiente
y los muebles guardando las distancias
y la composición que los hace armoniosos.

Naturalmente que la superficie
(de lo que sea) está pulida y limpia.
Y es también natural
que el polvo no se esconda en los rincones.

Pero hay algunas cosas
que provisionalmente coloqué aquí y allá
o que eché en el lugar de los trebejos.

Home Economics

This is the golden rule, the secret of order:
a place for everything
and everything in its place. That's how I've fixed my house.

An impeccable bookstand:
one shelf for the novels,
another for essays
and poetry on all the others

If you open a closet it smells of lavender
and you can't mistake the linen tablecloths
for the ones for daily use.

There's also the set of china for special occasions
and the other one that's used, broken, mismatched
and is never complete.

The clothes are in the right drawers
and the furniture is properly arranged
to make the room harmonious.

Naturally the tops
(of everything) are polished and clean.
It's also natural
that dust isn't hiding in the corners.

But there are some things I just put down here or there
or toss in the place I keep for catchalls.

Algunas cosas. Por ejemplo, un llanto
que no se lloró nunca;
una nostalgia de que me distraje,
un dolor, un dolor del que se borró el nombre,
un juramento no cumplido, una ansia
que se desvaneció como el perfume
de un frasco mal cerrado.

Y retazos de tiempo perdido en cualquier parte.

Esto me desazona. Siempre digo: mañana. . .
y luego olvido. Y muestro a las visitas,
orgullosa, una sala en la que resplandece
la regla de oro que me dió mi madre.

A few things. A cry, for example,
that was never cried,
a distracting nostalgia,
an ache, a pain whose name was blotted out,
a vow never kept, an anguish
that evaporated like perfume in
a partially closed bottle.

And remnants of time lost anywhere.

This discourages me. I always say, tomorrow . . .
and then forget. And proudly show company
a room that shines with the golden rule
my mother gave me.

(Translated by Maureen Ahern)

ULALUME GONZALEZ DE LEON considers herself Mexican even though she was born in Uruguay in 1932. For many years she has lived in Mexico City where she serves on the advisory board of the literary magazine. *Vuelta.* Her poems have appeared in a numer of magazines and have been collected in four volumes: *Plagio* (1973), *Ciel entier* (a selection of her poems translated into French and with a preface by Octavio Paz, 1978), *Plagio II* (1980), and *Viajes* (1983). In addition to poems, she has written short stories and essays and has published translations into Spanish of the poems of e.e. cummings, Ted Hughes, Elizabeth Bishop, Guillaume Apollinaire, as well as the suppressed wasp episode from Lewis Carroll's *Through the Looking Glass.* Octavio Paz calls her poems "aerial geometry." He says of them: "If we try to touch them, they disappear. Ulalume's poetry does not touch: it sees. A poetry for seeing. Objects, purified by her intellectual vision, attenuate until they become the lines of a sketch." He adds that, for Ulalume, "memory invents chimerical passages that are immediately dissipated by the poet's lucid gaze. Is vision, then, resolved in nonvision; is not-seeing the true seeing? Or, in the manner of negative theology, is poetic knowledge the supreme ignorance? Clearly it is a poetry for seeing—not realities but ideas, not ideas but forms, undulations, echoes. For seeing what remains from ideas, what remains from reality." In the fall of 1983, she was writer-in-residence in New York City under the sponsorship of the Center for Inter-American Relations.

Las sábanas familiares

En su cuarto blanco
entre blancas sabanas
se ha dormido
                y sueña
que duerme y que sueña
en su cuarto blanco

Se sabe soñando
porque de su cuerpo
a su cuerpo cae
infinitamente
y sin movimiento

Y de pronto llega
al fondo del cuerpo
y entonces despierta
en un cuarto rojo
dentro de su sueño

Sabe que despierta
dentro de su sueño
porque es rojo el cuarto
rojo todo blanco;
sábanas y cuerpo

Y otra vez se duerme
en su sueño
                y sueña
que en su cuarto blanco
dormido se encuentra
soñando que está
en un cuarto rojo
donde duerme y sueña

Familiar Sheets

In his white room
between white sheets
he's fallen asleep
                and dreams
that he sleeps and dreams
in his white room

He knows he's dreaming
because he falls
from his body to his body
infinitely
and motionless

And suddenly arrives
in the depths of his body
and then wakes
in a red room
inside his dream

He knows he wakes
inside his dream
because the room is red
everything white: red
sheets and body

Again he sleeps
in his dream
                and dreams
that he finds himself asleep
in his white room
dreaming that he's
in a red room
where he sleeps and dreams

Se sabe soñando
porque de su cuerpo
a su cuerpo cae
y del blanco al rojo
y del rojo al blanco
infinitamente
y sin movimiento

Y de pronto llega
al fondo del cuerpo
al fondo del sueño
al sueño sin fondo
a las familiares
sábanas de frío
al sueño de nadie

)Parentesis(

La vida está entre paréntesis
como la única parte cierta
de la frase de nunca acabar

El amor está entre paréntesis
como la única parte cierta
de la frase de la vida

Pero los paréntesis del amor
se abren al reves
          son
paréntesis para escapar
paréntesis para ir
a habitar el color verde

He knows he's dreaming
because he falls
from his body to his body
and from white to red
and from red to white
infinitely
and motionless

And suddenly arrives
in the depths of his body
the depths of the dream
the dream without depth
the familiar
sheets of coldness
nobody's dream

(Translated by Sara Nelson)

)Parentheses(

Life lies between parentheses
like the single certain factor
of a sentence that never ends

Love lies between parentheses
like the single certain factor
of a life's sentence

But the parentheses of love
open backwards
                    are
parentheses for escape
parentheses for going off
to live in the color green

(Translated by Eliot Weinberger)

Mariposa amarilla

Dentro de la mañana la vida hace ruido
pero ruido adentro hay un espacio de silencio
y dentro del silencio hay un hombre
que escribe una historia gris

La ventana está abierta
                              pero él
escribe separado de la mañana
separado de algo vivo que ahora insiste
como desde el otro lado de un vidrio

de algo vivo y desobediente
que se asoma a la página desde ninguna parte
que otea el camino de tinta
donde dicen que no las palabras
. . .
Está cerca
              pero escondido
como la luz dentro de la luz
como la vida dentro de la vida

No elige ser aún
                      Se demora
en contingencia aguda
en desprendido movimiento
en amarillo que tiembla
Prueba un delgado compromiso
entre engaño y substancia:
                              alas

Pero en un ángulo del aire
cobra de improviso un aplomo

Se concentra en destello
contra oscuridades de hojas

Yellow Butterfly

Life makes noise within the morning
but within the noise there is a space of silence
and within the silence there is a man
writing a gray story

The window is open
                    but he
writes separated from the morning
separated from something living that now insists
as if from the other side of a windowpane

something living and disobedient
leaning over the page from nowhere
inspecting the path of ink
where words say *no*
. . .
It is close
            but hidden
like the light within light
like the life within life

but does not choose to be
                        It lingers
in detached movement
in acute possibility
in a yellow that trembles
It attempts a frail compromise
between deception and substance:
                            wings

But in a corner of the air
with sudden aplomb

it gathers into a flash
against darkness of leaves

*

Es del todo
                Dice que sí
. . .
Hay un retraso en la mano
que escribe
                una duda un temblor
                        Se filtra
en la ajenía del discurso gris
una palabra:
                mariposa
Hay una corrección amarilla al sentido

La página está escrita
La mañana regresa
desde el otro lado de un vidrio
El ruido toma el espacio de silencio

El hombre alza los ojos
hacia oscuridades de hojas
y mira una ausencia menuda

It wholly is
         It says *yes*
. . .
There is a delay in the hand
that writes
            a doubt a tremor
One word filters through the otherness
of the gray speech:
                    butterfly
There is a yellow correction to the meaning

The page is written
Morning returns
from the other side of a windowpane
Noise takes over the space of silence

The man raises his eyes
toward darkness of leaves
and watches a small absence

(Translated by Sara Nelson)

Discontinuidad

Un pájaro
mientras miras por la ventana
cómo toma enero en jardín

cruza el aire (y se lleva
prendida a su retina
tu imagen

y vuela tan aprisa
se aleja tantos años tantas leguas
que llega hasta un país hasta un invierno equivodado:

en su bosque nevado
entre azules del frío y del silencio
el lobo se detiene y escucha

mezclado a las mareas subterráneas
urdidoras de primavera
el remoto latido de tu corazón en este cuarto)

Te asomas entonces al jardín
(te inclinas sobre la distancia
recién abierta entre tú y tú

y tienes miedo
de cononcer el país de no estar juntos)
Un infinito instante

te espero (Cambia el pájaro de espacio
Pierde el lobo el rastro levísimo
de tus pies en la nieve) Te vuelves

hacia mí y entras en mis ojos
con el jardín y enero
y un mirlo que atraviesa el cielo blanco

Discontinuity

A bird,
while you watch through the window
how January takes the garden,

crosses the air (and carries off
your image
imprisoned in its retina

and flies so quickly
goes so many years so many leagues away
that it reaches a mistaken country a mistaken winter:

in its snowy wood
in the blueness of cold and silence
the wolf pauses and

joined in the subterranean tides
that plot spring he listens
to the remote beat of your blood in this room)

Then you peer into the garden
(you lean over the newly-opened
distance between you and you

and are afraid
to know the country of not being together)
A limitless moment

I wait for you (The bird changes spaces
the wolf loses the faint scent
of your tracks in the snow) You turn

toward me and enter my eyes
with the garden and January and
a blackbird moving through the white sky

(Translated by Sara Nelson)

Jardín escrito

En el jardín que recuerdo
sopla un viento que mueve las hojas
del jardín donde ahora
estoy escribiendo

En el jardín que imagino
sopla un viento que mueve las hojas
del jardín que recuerdo

Y en el jardín donde ahora
estoy escribiendo
sopla un viento que mueve las hojas
sin jardín:
      armisticio
de fronda imaginaria y fronda recordada

pero también las hojas verdes
del jardín donde escribo

pero también las hojas blancas
en que estoy escribiendo

y nace otro jardín

Written Garden

In the garden I remember
wind blows and shakes the leaves
in the garden where I'm writing

In the garden I imagine
wind blows and shakes the leaves
in the garden I remember

And in the garden where I'm writing
wind blows and shakes the leaves
without a garden:
                    a pact
between imagined and remembered leaf

but the green leaves too
in the garden where I write

but the white leaves too
where I'm writing

and another garden is born

(Translated by Eliot Weinberger)

CECILIA BUSTAMANTE was born in Lima, Peru, in 1932 and began to publish while still in her twenties. Her published books include *Altas hojas* (1956), *Símbolos del corazón* (1961), *Poesía* (1964), *Nuevos poemas y audiencia* (1965), *El nombre de las cosas* (1970), *Amor en Lima* (1977, and *Discernimiento* (1978). Besides writing poems, Bustamante has translated the work of U.S. poets into Spanish and has been active in organizing conferences and speeches about Peruvian life and literature, and especially about women writers. Her work has also been included in half a dozen collections of Peruvian poetry, published both in Peru and in Spain, and has been translated into English and French. The themes of her work are time, nature, memory, language. But her poems expound on the interrelationships of things and the ability of poetry to "penetrate experience and make it more real." Mirko Lauer says, "There is in the poetry of Cecilia Bustamante an alchemical vocation, attentive to the subterranean currents that through the natural elements run below everyday events. More than words to speak, hers are words to boast, to conjure, to penetrate essences. . . ." At present, Bustamante is living in this country and has no plans to return to Peru.

Bajo el sol

Una tarde como el hambre
como la soledad

Entre las manos destruyo roja sal
una arma plateada que no es un pez
una campanita sorda más bien
nos engaña como si fuera
un ñorbo estático
pero es el fuego
azul y blanco traidor
sospecho nada más.

Es una tarde de sol como un niño
alegre y cansado.
No sólo la arena existe no las playas
el sol me lo dice
también interiores tierras nuevas
el recuerdo el ansia la terracota
tierra en que seca el desvelo su llama.

A la izquierda el fuego
a la derecha
oh en mí misma incendio
el hambre de cubrir esta cicatriz
con la piel que me arranco.

Under the Sun

An afternoon like hunger
like solitude

Between my hands I break red salt
a silvered weapon that isn't a fish
more nearly a little deaf bell.
The afternoon beguiles us as if it were
an ecstatic passion flower
but I suspect it's fire
blue and white traitor
nothing more.

It is an afternoon sunny
as a happy and tired child.
The sun tells us
not only sand exists or beaches
also new lands of the interior
memory anxiety terracota
earth in which longing dries its flame.

To the left fire
to the right
and in me my own fire
hunger to hide this scar
with the skin I tear off.

(Translated by Mary Crow)

Resonancias

Rojos días
también arman de navajas
las canciones
también siembran
ríos
con sus cuerdas
de metal afilado.

Y las cenas como antaño.
La delgada madera
marcada con harina
y sabrosa hora amarilla
de poca luz y puños cerrados
alimento sobre la mesa
tímidos amigos de otro tiempo
jinetes guitarras instrumentos
colgados para siempre
a partir de nosotros
somos los mismos
sobre las mismas raíces
rondamos alrededor
de la terca cena violentada.

Las canciones
nos dejan ahogándonos
pidiendo misericordia
desde estos trajes oscuros
desde estos rostros oscuros
en esa casa oscura.
Resonancias.

Resonances

Red days
also arm the songs
with razors
& sow rivers
with their chords
of keen metal.

Supper like long ago
the thin wood
stained with flour
& the savoury yellow
twilight & closed fists
food on the table
shy friends from another time
horsemen guitars instruments
hung forever
yet we're the same
above the same roots
we patrol the outskirts
of the stubborn disrupted supper.

The songs
leave us drowning
& begging for mercy
from these dark suits
& dark faces
in this dark house.
Resonances.

(Translated by David Tipton)

Despierta

Zumba la abeja de la noche
retumbando
en las galerías del sueño
entre las abundantes hojas
que ha derribado el día.

Entre realidades
zumba
más allá del terror
por aquellas horas mejores
en viñedos
de desolada memoria.
Zumba, devora
y con su sonido descubre
al cuerpo que declina
mientras arde el fuego
mejor de los cielos.

Se acumula en la mente,
instruye al gorrión,
a los gordos buitres,
al buey que muge
en las trampas que hieden
en los ojos del orgullo
en sus torpes paisajes
que reverberan vanamente.

El que preste oídos
encontrará discernimiento
y no sólo ceniza o traición
Pues este zumbido es el vuelo
al otro lado del tiempo
que no se puede acallar.

Awake

The bee of night hums
among abundant leaves
resounding
in the galleries of dream
that have demolished day.

Among realities
through those best hours
it hums
beyond terror
in vineyards
of desolate memory.
It hums, devours
and with its sound discovers
the body that diminishes
while the fire of the skies
burns brighter.

It accumulates in the mind,
instructs the sparrow,
the fat vultures,
the ox that bellows
in the swamps that stink
in the eyes of pride
in its torpid landscapes
that reverberate in vain.

He who lends his ears
will find understanding
and not only ash or betrayal.
Because this humming
that cannot be hushed
is the flight
to the other side of time.

(Translated by Mary Crow)

El astronauta

Tengo una hermosa estructura en el corazón,
delicadas venas de mercurio,
una máquina perfecta en el árbol de la vida.
Soy un campo de electrodos, de chispas azules,
de grafismos autónomos, de cordiales silencios.
Soy una perla
cuando me desnudan para el vuelo.

Será como lanzarme en tus brazos
y abatirme en tus estrellas,
tus radiaciones, tus misterios.
Será tomarte nuevamente
en mi red plena de alas.

¡Estoy listo en todos los idiomas,
para lanzarme lejos de tí!
¡Estoy sereno en todos los dialectos,
para contemplar invisibles barreras
controladas con rayos presurosos—
desde mi cápsula. ¡Oh, corazón!
Yo soy la oruga extraña
que flota entre banderas desplegadas
de mi siglo a los años por venir.

The Astronaut

I have a beautiful structure in my heart,
fine veins of mercury,
a perfect machine in the tree of life.
I am a field of electrodes, blue sparks,
of autonomous sketchings, of comfortable silences.
I am a pearl
when they undress me for the flight.

It will be as if I launched myself into your arms
and set myself adrift among your stars,
your radiations, your mysteries.
It will be to take you again
into my net full of wings.

I am ready in all languages
to launch myself far from you!
I am calm in all the dialects—
contemplating invisible barriers
controlled by pressurized rays
from my capsule!
Oh, heart! I am the foreign rocket
floating among hoisted flags
from my years to the centuries to come.

(Translated by Mary Crow)

Born in 1927 in Santiago de Chile of immigrant parents, RAQUEL JODOROWSKY has lived for many years in Peru and is now generally regarded as a Peruvian poet. Her poems reveal "something of the hallucinated world of Franz Kafka and something of the telluric sadness of the Pole Bruno Schulz, . . . who died in the crematory ovens of the German Nazis. This world of torments, sufferings, and screams that comes from the depth of the centuries is . . . the characteristic element of this woman who is all poet." But there is another side to Raquel Jodorowsky which writes poems of love and tenderness and which flirts with the sentimental. The two sides often move together in a poetry that is painfully bittersweet and strange. Her poems, which have been published in many magazines in most of the countries of the continent, are collected in *Dimensión de los días* (1950), *Aposento y época* (1952), *La ciudad inclemente* (1957), *En la pared de los sueños alguien llama* (1957), *El sentido inverso* (1962), *Alnico y Kemita, Cantata del espacio* (1964), *El Ajy Tojen* (1964), *Mi casa abrakadabra* (1970), and *El caramelo del sol* (1978). In the last half dozen years she has been concentrating on her painting and has been showing her work in galleries in Lima; her art work, like her poetry, is full of a child's vision of the world with its unexpected proportions and colors, its innocence and directness. Last year she published a new book of poems, *Lo que llama desde la eternidad—Chavin de Hauntar*.

Canción para cuerdas de garganta e instrumentos de llanto electrónico

Ruidos del universo circulando en mi intestino
Ruidos de máquinas masticando hombres
Ruidos de trajes aniquilando cuerpos
Ruidos de botas hundiendo ojos que sueñan
Ruidos de héroes vistiéndose con la piel de sus enemigos
Riudos de niños devorando abuelos
Ruidos de microbios abatiendo hígados
Ruidos de gargantas tratando de cantar mientras esperan
　　en una silla eléctrica
Ruidos de blancos cazadores de cabezas negras
Ruidos de alfileres desinflando estómagos de banqueros de
　　150 kilos
Ruidos de uñas escalando cárceles
Ruidos de falos rompiendo tímpanos
Ruidos de lluvia lluvia lluvia cayendo cayendo sobre un
　　cuerpo que se desangra sin ayuda
Ruidos de escritores mordiendo escritores
Ruidos de abadías ahogando espíritus
Ruidos de políticos conservándose en saliva
Ruidos de genios vaciándose en reservados
Ruidos de hambre aullando en la soledad de hospitales
Ruidos de criminales que subieron al cielo inmortalizándose
　　en estampas
Ruidos de poemas quemados por el estado
Ruidos de familias que se separaron se buscaron se llamaron
　　se tragaron sus ecos sin respuesta dentro de hornos
　　crematorios
Ruidos de libros de profesores anunciando los progresos de la civilización
Ruidos de mi mirada persiguiéndome en la oscuridad
Ruidos de ruidos de ruidos rodando en el vacío en
　　el silencio en el vacío.

Song for Vocal Chords and Instruments of Electronic Crying

Sound of the universe flowing in my intestines
Sounds of machines chewing up men
Sounds of clothes annihilating bodies
Sounds of boots kicking in eyes that dream
Sounds of heroes dressing in their enemies' skin
Sounds of children devouring grandparents
Sounds of microbes battering livers
Sounds of throats trying to sing while waiting
    in the electric chair
Sounds of white hunters of black heads
Sounds of pins deflating stomachs of 200 pound
    bankers
Sounds of fingers scaling prison walls
Sounds of penises breaking drums
Sound of rain rain rain falling falling on a
    body that is bleeding without help
Sounds of writers gnawing writers
Sounds of priests smothering spirits
Sounds of politicians being preserved in saliva
Sounds of genuises being drained in compounds
Sounds of hunger howling in the solitude of hospitals
Sound of criminals that went to heaven immortalized
    on posters
Sounds of poems burned by the state
Sounds of families that were separated searched for each other
    called to each other swallowed their unanswered echoes
    inside crematories
Sounds of teachers' books announcing the advances of
    civilization
Sounds of my eyes following me in the darkness
Sounds of sounds of sounds circling in the vacuum in
    the silence in the vacuum.

(Translated by Pamela Carmell)

Malaguas

El mar entrega
flores de vidrio
como luz espesa.
Son geografías transparentes.
Los hombres dicen
que parecen animales
y les ponen agrios nombres.
En medio de ninguna parte
el mar ofrece
un jardin de pétalos
de carne de agua dura.
Los hombres despedazan
estos ojos submarinos
en la arena
clavan palos
en las rosas moradas
piedras líquidas
destruyendo en su fondo
una ciudad del universo
reflejada.
El hombre corazón de ídolo
pies de cemento
no descubre.
¿Cómo pretende dar
si no sabe recibir?
El mar
todo su azul un yacimiento de plata!
recoge los vestigios
del esplendor
desatado en las orillas.
Vuelve a sí mismo
con su cosecha quebrada
y entrega a los hombres
en silencio
una mañana
que lucha
contra el alma.

Jellyfish

The sea offers up
flowers of glass
like thick light.
They are transparent landscapes.
Men say
they are like animals
and give them bitter names.
Out of the middle of nowhere
the sea offers
a garden of petals
flesh of hard water.
Men tear these underwater eyes
to pieces
in the sand
drive sticks
into deep purple roses
liquid rocks
destroying at its foundation
a city of the universe
reflected.
Man heart of an idol
feet of concrete
does not see.
How can he claim to give
if he does not know how to receive?
The sea
all its blue, lode of silver!
gathers up its vestiges
of splendor
unraveled on the shore.
It retreats
with its broken harvest
and renders to men
in silence
a morning
that wars
with the soul.

(Translated by Pamela Carmell)

Poema en todos los idiomas

Tu sexo era mi Patria
el territorio de mi muerte
Tu sexo era mi espejo
una palabra prohibida
un animal de invernadero
un profeta evangélico
Donde llegaban mis cabellos
para aprender a caminar
Tu sexo la puerta del universo
desde donde me río
Tu sexo que a veces me equivoco
y escribo la palabra saxofón
La boca surrealista
para decir: Yo te amo
Tu sexo sin cuerpo
vestido de piel
El fondo de una noche blanca
donde me pongo y me saco los ojos
Tu sexo que se avergüenza del día
Tu sexo para cambiar de planeta
Tu sexo sin evolución, espada exterminadora
Rey de los fósiles, tu sexo
el triunfo de los mamíferos
la lágrima que establece un verano
de 30 millones de años
Tu sexo mi Biblia
mi Dios mal interpretado
Un viaje sub-marino
Tu sexo para descubrir
el principio del alma

Poem in Every Language

Your sex was my Fatherland
region of my death
Your sex was my mirror
forbidden word
wintering animal
evangelical prophet
Where my hair finally
learned to walk
Your sex door of the universe
where I mock myself
Your sex I can mistake
and write the word saxophone
The surrealistic mouth
for saying: I love you
Your bodiless sex
dressed in fur
Depths of white night
where I sit and take out my eyes
Your sex shamed by the day
Your sex moving the heavens
Your sex unevolved, exterminating sword
King of the fossils, your sex
the triumph of mammals
tear that began a summer
of 30 million years
Your sex my Bible
my God misunderstood
Voyage through the deep
Your sex for discovering
the source of my soul

(Translated by Pamela Carmell)

El poder del hombre

Cuando el poderío del hombre
se aquieta
detiene sus máquinas
guarda las armas
Surge un silencio
donde oigo
la luz de la Luna.
Un químico silencio
donde veo los ruidos
del comienzo de la Tierra.
En él siento crecer
las espaldas del tiempo
crepitando como insectos quebrados.
Son ciertas horas
fuera de las horas
que comienzo a balancearme
sobre el horizonte.
En el borde del planeta
capto la poesía dictada
en otras órbitas.
No es la quietud de la naturaleza
donde los animales cantan o se llaman.
Es el silencio de la mente
que nos entrega
a la magia del Mundo.

The Power of Man

When the force of man
calms down
stops its machines
puts away arms
a silence swells
in which I hear
the light of the Moon.
A chemical silence
in which I see sounds
from the beginnings of Earth.
In this, I feel growing
the spine of time
crackling like broken insects.
These are hours
apart from the hours
when I start to balance myself
on the horizon.
On the edge of the planet
I capture poetry
dictated in other orbits.
It is not the stillness of nature
in which animals sing or call to each other.
It is the silence of the mind
that leads us
to the magic of the World.

(Translated by Pamela Carmell)

CLARIBEL ALEGRIA was born in Estelí, Nicaragua, on May 12, 1924. Her family moved to El Salvador when she was only nine months old and she grew up there. She was educated in Santa Ana, El Salvador, and later attended George Washington University. After traveling widely and living in various countries of South America and Europe, she settled in Mallorca, Spain, in 1966 with her husband and translator, Darwin J. Flakoll, and her four children. Author of more than fifteen books, some of them in collaboration with her husband, Alegría has written novels, short stories, children's stories, as well as poems. In addition, she has edited several anthologies and is a widely published translator. Her books of poems include *Anillo de silencio* (1948), *Suite* (1951), *Vigilias* (1953), *Acuario* (1955), *Huésped de mi tiempo* (1961), *Vía Unica* (1965), *Aprendizaje* (1970), *Pagaré a Cobrar* (1973), *Sobrevivo* (1978), and *Suma y sigue* (1981). In 1982, she published a short novel, *Album familiar*. Her work has been translated into 11 different languages, and a collection of her poems was translated into English by Carolyn Forché under the title *Flowers from the Volcano* (University of Pittsburgh Press, 1982). She has herself translated both poems and novels, from English into Spanish and from Spanish into English. Currently she is working in Nicaragua, with husband, on two books: *El derecho a cantar,* about political prisoners in El Salvador, and a second book, not yet titled, about Central America during the Reagan epoch. In a poem entitled "Personal Creed," she has written, "I believe in my people/ who have been exploited for five hundred years," and also, "I believe in the blue cows of Chagall." It is this union of art and social protest that typifies her work at its best.

Flores del volcán

A Roberto y Ana María

Catorce volcanes se levantan
en mi país memoria
en mi país de mito
que día a día invento
catorce volcanes de follaje y piedra
donde nubes extrañas se detienen
y a veces el chillido
de un pájaro extraviado.
¿Quién dijo que era verde mi país?
es más rojo
es más gris
es más violento:
el Izalco que ruge
exigiendo más vidas
los eternos chacmol
que recogen la sangre
y los que beben sangre
del chacmol
y los huérfanos grises
y el volcán babeando
toda esa lava incandescente
y el guerrillero muerto
y los mil rostros traicionados
y los niños que miran
para contar la historia.
No nos quedó ni un reino
uno a uno cayeron
a lo largo de América
el acero sonaba
en los palacios
en las calles
en los bosques
y saqueaban el templo
los centauros
y se alejaba el oro
y se sigue alejando
en barcos yanquis

Flowers from the Volcano

To Roberto and Ana Maria

Fourteen volcanoes rise
in my remembered country,
in my mythical country
that day by day I invent.
Fourteen volcanoes of foliage and stone
where strange clouds linger
and sometimes the screech
of a homeless bird.
Who said that my country was green?
It is more red,
more gray,
more violent:
Izalco roars,
demanding more lives.
The eternal Chacmools
who collect the blood
and those who drink the blood
offered by the Chacmools,
and the gray orphans
and the volcanoes drooling
all this incandescent lava
and the dead guerilla,
the thousand betrayed faces,
the children who are watching
so that they can tell the story.
Not one kingdom was left us.
One by one they fell
all over America.
Steel rang
in palaces
in streets
in forests
and the centaurs
sacked the temple,
and the gold disappeared
and continues to disappear
aboard yankee ships,

el oro del café
mezclado con la sangre
mezclado con el látigo
y la sangre.
El sacerdote huía
dando gritos
en medio de la noche
convocaba a sus fieles
y abrían el pecho de un guerrero
para ofrecerle al Chac
su corazón humeante.
Nadie cree en Izalco
que Tlaloc esté muerto
por más televisores
heladeras
toyotas
el ciclo ya se acerca
es extraño el silencio del volcán
desde que dejó de respirar
Centroamérica tiembla
se derrumbó Managua
se hundió la tierra en Guatemala
el huracán Fifi
arrasó con Honduras
dicen que los yanquis lo desviaron
que iba hacia Florida
y lo desviaron
el oro del café
desembarca en New York
allí lo tuestan
lo trituran
lo envasan
y le ponen un precio.
«Siete de junio
noche fatal
bailando el tango
la capial»
Desde la terraza ensombrecida
se domina el volcán San Salvador
lo suben por los flancos
mansiones de dos pisos
protegidas por muros

the golden coffee
stained with blood
stained with whip
and blood.
The priest fled
screaming;
in the middle of the night
he gathered the faithful
and they opened a warrior's breast
to offer to Chac
his steaming heart.
No one believes in Izalco
that Tlaloc is dead
in spite of television
refrigerators
Toyotas.
The cycle is closing.
Strange the volcano's silence.
Since it stopped breathing
Central America is trembling.
Managua crumbled,
the earth sank in Guatemala,
Hurricane Fifi
flattened Honduras.
They say the yankees diverted it,
that it was moving toward Florida
and they turned it aside.
The golden coffee
is unloaded in New York
where they roast it,
grind it,
can it,
give it a price.
Siete de Junio
noche fatal
bailando el tango
la capital.
San Salvador's volcano
looms above the shady terraces.
Two-story mansions
protected by walls
four meters high

de cuatro metros de alto
le suben rojas y jardines
con rosas de Inglaterra
y araucarias enanas
y pinos de Uruguay
un poco más arriba
ya en el cráter
hundidos en el cráter
viven gentes del pueblo
que cultivan sus flores
y envían a sus niños a venderlas.
El ciclo ya se acerca
las flores cuscatlecas
se llevan bien con la ceniza
crecen grandes y fuertes
y lustrosas
bajan los niños del volcán
bajan como la lava
con sus ramos de flores
como raíces bajan
como ríos
se va acercando el ciclo
los que viven en casas de dos pisos
protegidas del robo por los muros
se asoman al balcón
ven esa ola roja
que desciende
y ahogan en whisky su temor
sólo son pobres niños
con flores del volcán
con jacintos
y pascuas
y mulatas
pero crece la ola
que se los va a tragar
porque el chacmol de turno
sigue exigiendo sangre
porque se acerca el ciclo
porque Tlaloc no ha muerto.

march up its flanks,
grillwork gates and gardens
with roses from England,
dwarf araucarias,
Uruguayan pines.
Farther up in the crater,
in the very pit of the crater
live peasant families
who cultivate flowers
and send their children to sell them.
The cycle is closing.
Cuscatlecan flowers
thrive
in volcanic ash.
They grow strong,
tall, brilliant.
the volcano's children flow down,
flow down the sides like lava
with their bouquets of flowers,
meandering down like roots,
like rivers.
The cycle is closing.
Dwellers in two-story houses
protected from thieves by walls
peer from their balconies,
see the red wave
descending
and they drown their fears in whiskey.
They are only children in rags
with flowers from the volcano,
with *jacintos*
and *pascuas*
and *mulatas.*
The wave is swelling,
the devouring wave,
because today's chacmool
still demands blood,
because the cycle is closing,
because Tlaloc is not dead.

(Translated by Darwin J. Flakoll)

Soy espejo

Brilla el agua
en mi piel
y no la siento
corre a chorros el agua
por mi espalda
no la siento
me froto con la toalla
me pellizco en un brazo
no me siento
aterrada me miro en el espejo
ella también se pincha
comienzo a vestirme
a tropezones
de los rincones brotan
relámpagos de gritos
ojos desorbitados
ratas que corren
dientes
aun no siento nada
me extravió en las calles;
niños con caras sucias
pidiéndome limosna
muchachas prostitutas
que no tienen quince años
todo es llaga en las calles
tanques que se aproximan
bayonetas alzadas
cuerpos que caen
llanto
por fin siento mi brazo
dejé de ser fantasma
me duele
luego existo
vuelvo a mirar la escena:
muchachos que corren
desangrados
mujeres con pánico
en el rostro

I'm a Mirror

The water glistens
on my skin
and I don't feel it
The water streams
down my back
I don't feel it
I towel myself
pinch my own arm
feel nothing
terrified, I stare into the mirror
she pinches herself
I start dressing hastily
in the corners appear
crazed eyes
glints of screams
scurrying rats
teeth
still I feel nothing
I wander through streets:
dirty-faced children
begging for pennies
teen-aged prostitutes
the streets are running sores
rumbling tanks
flashing bayonets
bodies falling
the sound of sobbing
I finally feel my arm
I've stopped being a phantom
I hurt
therefore I exist
I look again at the scene:
boys who run
bleeding
women with panic
in their faces

esta vez duele menos
me pellizco de nuevo
y ya no siento nada
simplemente reflejo
lo que pasa a mi lado
los tanques
no son tanques
ni los gritos
son gritos
soy un espejo plano
en que nada penetra
mi superficie
es dura
es brillante
es pulida
me convertí en espejo
y estoy descarnada
apenas si conservo
una memoria vaga
del dolor.

now it hurts less
I pinch myself again
now I feel nothing
I simple reflect
what happens around me
the tanks
aren't tanks
and the screams
aren't screams
I'm a flat mirror
in which nothing penetrates
my suface
is hard
brillant
polished
I've turned into a mirror
I am bloodless
I scarcely retain
a vague memory
of pain.

(Translated by Darwin J. Flakoll)

Tamalitos de Cambray

(4 millones 200 mil tamalitos)
*—A Eduardo y Helena que me pidieron
una receta salvadoreña—*

Dos libras de masa de mestizo
media libra de lomo gachupín
cocido y bien picado
una cajita de pasas beatas
dos cucharadas de leche de Malinche
una taza de agua bien rabiesa
un sofrito con cascos de conquistadores
tres cebollas jesuitas
una bolsita de oro multinacional
dos dientes de dragón
una zanahoria presidencial
dos cucharadas de alcahuetes
manteca de indios de Panchimalco
dos tomates ministeriales
media taza de azúcar televisora
dos gotas de lava del volcán
siete hojas de pito
(no seas malpensado es somnífero)
lo pones todo a cocer
a fuego lento
por quinientos años
y verás qué sabor.

Little Cambric Tamales

(Makes 4,200,00 tamales)
—For Eduardo and Helena who asked me
for a Salvadorean recipe—

Two pounds of mestizo dough
a half-pound of loin of overseer
well-minced and cooked
a box of devout raisins
two tablespoons of Malinche milk
one cup of rabid water
a fry of conquistador helmets
three Jesuit onions
a small bag of multinational gold
two dragon's teeth
one presidential carrot
two tablespoons of political pimps
lard of Panchimalco Indians
two ministerial tomatoes
a half-cup of television sugar
two drops of volcanic lava
seven leaves of *pito*
(don't be dirty-minded; they're somniferous)
put everything to boil
over a slow fire
for five hundred years
and you'll see what a flavor it has!

(Translated by Darwin J. Flakoll)

CIRCE MAIA was born in 1932 in Montevideo, Uruguay, and now lives in Tacuarembó, where she teaches French literature at the Alliance Française and studies German and modern Greek. When she has mastered Greek, she would like to translate the poems of Odysseus Elytis into Spanish. Her first book of poems, *Plumitas,* was published when she was 11. Since then, she has published five books of poetry: *En el tiempo* (1958), *Presencia diaria* (1964), *El puente* (1970), *Cambios, permanencias* (1978), and *Dos voces* (1981). Her poetry has been described as "direct" and "open," "written in a conversational tone but with greater intensity." It uses daily experience but makes that experience seem anything but ordinary; suddenly the daily world comes alive with a mystery that is full of potential for terror but also for beauty. Deeply philosophical, her poetry "moves with pleasure and power among things and reveals the poet's exceptional ability to situate herself in the nucleus of little conflicts, of imperceptible doubts, and to illuminate through detail. . .these surroundings deliberately minimal."

Donde había barrancas

Otra vez se levanta de la memoria el golpe
del remo contra el agua. Brilla el arroyo y tiemblan
las hojas en la sombra.

Miran ojos risueños, pelo mojado. Arriba
azul y sol y azul. . . Mira los troncos negros
y rotos, oye el agua.

Tibia madera siento todavía en la mano
y a cada golpe sordo que da ahora mi sangre
se vuelve a hundir el remo en verde frío y algas.

Un tallo firme y verde venía enero alzando.
Y venían del viento, del amor, y venían
de la vida
alas rojas y en vuelo, los días del verano.
      Rema, remero
      y no escuches el golpe
      negro, del remo.
El golpe corta trozos cortos de tiempo
trozos iguales, casi relojería
y se piensa que adonde se van cayendo
un golpe y otro golpe junto al vuelo del día.

Mira que se ennegrecen las blancas horas
y de querer pararlas ya casi duelen.

Caen al alma fríos y de ceniza
los golpes que en el agua dieron los remos.

Y atrás se ve la cara tersa del río
el rostro del verano, azul y liso.

Where There Used to be Badlands

Again there rises from memory the beat
of the oar against the water. The stream shines and leaves
tremble in the shadow.

Wet hair, smiling eyes look. Above,
blue and sun and blue. . . Look at the black
and broken tree trunks, listen to the water.

I still feel warm wood in my hand
and at each dull beat which my blood makes now
the oar again sinks into the green cold and algae.

A firm and green stem came raising January
and there came from the wind, from love, and there came
from life
red wings in flight, the days of summer.
>   Row, rower
>   and don't listen to the black
>   beat of the oar.
The beat cuts short slices of time
equal slices, almost like the work of the watchmaker
and you think of whereever they go falling
one beat and another beat with the flight of the day.

Look how the white hours grow black
and how they almost ache from trying to stop.

The beats fall on the soul cold and ashen
the beats which the oars made on the water.

And behind you can see the terse face of the river
the face of summer, blue and flat.

(Translated by Patsy Boyer and Mary Crow)

Posibilidades

Hemos resuelto no existir. Mejor dicho
se ha resuelto que no existiéramos.
Así quedamos quietos, en el fondo,
sin hacer nada.

Como niños demasiado buenos
que han renunciado al juego por no hacer ruido
y ni hablar ni leer, porque hay crujidos
al dar vuelta las hojas.

Adelgazados, sí, casi sin peso,
sin movernos, ya dijo.
Sólo queda mirar a quien no mira,
no nos ve casi nunca.

¡Pero a veces!

A veces existimos todavía
en forma de punzadas silenciosas.
Un pensamiento-aguja, voz-astilla
da el inaudible grito: "¡Todavía!"

Possibilities

We have resolved not to exist. Or rather
it has been resolved that we not exist.
So we stay quiet, deep down,
doing nothing.

Like children too good
who have quit playing in order not to make noise
and neither talk nor read because there are rustlings
when the pages turn.

Thin, yes, almost without weight,
without moving ourselves, as I said.
Only, we remain looking at someone who doesn't look,
who almost never sees us.

But sometimes!

Sometimes we still exist
in the form of silent stabs.
A thought-needle, voice-splinter
utters the inaudible scream: "Still!"

(Translated by Patsy Boyer and Mary Crow)

Mojadas uvas. . .

Mojadas uas, aire de vacaciones,
sobre la palma de la mano, como un trompo girando
lavado, puro y negro corazón de la noche.

Qué a compás con nosotros su latido de tiempo
y cómo se sentía la dicha a veces, fuerte
densa, casi tangible
no se sabía dónde.

Al oner el mantel sobre la mesa, estaba
hecha de tela blanca o era de vidrio y loza
y en la cena, volaba
de un lado a otro, sobre
la luz de las miradas
de un vaso a un mueble, del pan al agua.

Se oía su latido
en las conversaciones
en los acogedores silencios, en saludos
en su: hasta mañana!

Ahora
se han ido a acostar todos
y como nunca más ha vuelto a levantarse
la mirada risueña,

se volaron las noches de diciembre y el brillo
de las frutas lavadas
se volaron los rápidos pasos en la vereda
y aquella que venía
—no se sabe de dónde—
dicha, ráfaga oscura
en la piel de la cara.

Wet Grapes. . .

Wet grapes, vacation air,
across the palm of the hand, like a top twirling
washed, pure and black heart of night.

How in tune with us its beat in time
and how we felt happiness sometimes, strong
thick, almost tangible
no one knew from where.

Putting the cloth on the table,
we noticed it was made of white cloth
or it was glass and pottery
and during supper it flew
from one side to the other, over
the light of the glances
of a glass at a table, or bread and water.

One heard its beat
in the conversations
in the comfortable silence, in greetings
in the: see you tomorrow!

Now
everyone has gone off to bed
and as if the smiling glance
would never get up again,

the December nights flew away and the shine
of unwashed fruits
the quick steps on the path flew away
and the one who was coming
—who knows from where—
happiness, dark gust
on the skin of the face.

(Translated by Patsy Boyer and Mary Crow)

Vámonos de nuevo

Tierra húmeda y negra de las barrancas
y raíces, al lado mismo del agua.
—Saltos sobre las piedras
y remolinos
hay hojas navegantes
y brillo, y frío.—

Una piedra lustrosa, negra y lisa
un reflejo de troncos, de pastos altos
de ramas finas
y una voz rumorosa de viento en hojas
diciendo algo confuso, sobre nuestras cabezas.

Flores muy chicas
con pétalos que arrojan un rojo vivo
y casi alumbran.

Alas de insectos
de un celeste que casi no es color, transparente
tiemblan, se agitan.

Y aquel rumor de monte, de vida múltiple
latiendo en cada hueco, en cada grieta,
aquel ruido de viento, de agua
de pájaros alzando el vuelo
con un golpe de ala y un grito áspero.

Let's Go Again

Black damp earth of the badlands
and roots, by the very edge of the water.
—Leaping over the stones
and eddies
there are sailing leaves
and brilliance, and cold.—

A shining stone, black and smooth
a reflection of tree trunks, of high pastures
of delicate branches
and a gossiping voice of wind in leaves
saying something confused, above our heads.

Tiny flowers
with petals which cast a glowing red
and almost shed light.

Insect wings
of a sky blue almost not color, transparent
tremble, flutter.

And that rumor of wilderness, of multiple life
beating in each hollow, in each cleft,
that sound of wind, of water
or birds taking flight
with a blow of wing and a bitter scream.

(Translated by Patsy Boyer and Mary Crow)

Vendrá un viento del sur

Vendrá un viento del sur con lluvia desatada
a golpear en las puertas cerradas y en los vidrios
a golpear en los rostros de agrios gestos.

Vendrán alegres oleajes ruidosos
subiendo las veredas y calles silenciosas
por el barrio del puerto.

Que se lave la cara la ciudad endurecida
sus piedras y maderas polvorientas, raídas
su corazón sombrío.

Que por lo menos haya asombro en las opacas
miradas taciturnas.
Y que muchos se asusten y los niños se rían
y el verdor de la luz del agua nos despierte
nos bañe, nos persiga.

Que nos dé por correr y abrazarnos
que se abran las puertas de todas las casas
y salga la gente
por las escaleras, desde los balcones
llamándose. . .

A Wind Will Come from the South

A wind will come from the south with unleashed rain
to beat on closed doors and on the windows
to beat on faces with bitter expressions.

Happy noisy waves will come
climbing paths and silent streets
through the port district.

Let the hardened city wash its face
its stones and dusty wood, worn out
its heart sombre.

Let there be surprise at least in the opaque
taciturn glances.
And let many people be frightened, and the children laugh
and the greenness of the water's light wake us
bathe us, follow us.

Let it make us run and embrace each other
and let the doors of all the houses open
and the people come out
down the stairs, from the balconies,
calling to each other. . .

(Translated by Patsy Boyer and Mary Crow)

MARIA SABINA represents the women seers of Latin America who, in the present and in the past, have composed their poetry in the name of religions both native and colonial or blends of both. With the approval of the community and perhaps the assistance of a local hallucinogen, such shamanesses could boast of their own powers (often real enough in the realms of herbal medicine and natural healing) without offending male standards of femininity for the power they claimed was "divine." Thus, Maria Sabina attributes her song and her power to god, and to the mushrooms, the "children," which give her the sacred gift of language. However "pagan" these last words sound, Maria Sabina is a Catholic, baptized in the Catholic church March 17, 1894, in Huautla, Mexico, several days after her birth. Her life has been recorded by Alvaro Estrada in *Maria Sabina: Her Life and Chants,* the source of the chants used in this anthology. The original chants in Mazatec were first recorded in the 1950's by R. Gordon Wasson (see his Folkways record and his book, *Maria Sabina and Her Mazatec Mushroom Velada*). Today her chant retains its freshness and its appeal. It is full of a childlike wonder and slyness. The modernity of its power led poet Ann Waldman to adapt it as her model in *Fast Speaking Woman.* Melody and matter both charm—and so the endless chant becomes fitting epigraph and end to this anthology.

I Just Lightning

I just lightning, says
I just shout, says
I just whistle, says
I am a lawyer woman, says
I am a woman of transactions, says
Holy Father, says
That is his clock, says
That is his lord eagle, says
That is his opossum, says
That is his lord hawk, says
Holy Father, says
Mother, says
I am a mother woman beneath the water, says
I am a woman wise in medicine, says
Holy Father, says
I am a saint woman, says
I am a spirit woman, says
She is woman of light, says
She is woman of the day, says
Holy Father, says
I am a shooting star woman, says
I am a shooting star woman, says
I am a whirling woman of colors, says
I am a whirling woman of colors, says
I am a clean woman, says
I am a clean woman, says
I am a woman who whistles, says
I am a woman who looks into the insides of things, says
I am a woman who investigates, says
I am a woman wise in medicine, says
I am a mother woman, says
I am a spirit woman, says
I am a woman of light, says
I am a woman of the day, says
I am a Book woman, says
I am a woman who looks into the insides of things, says

(Translated from the Mazatec to Spanish by Eloina Estrada de González
and from Spainsh to English by Henry Munn)